INSECTS
OF THE
WORLD

INSECTS
OF THE
WORLD

Anthony Wootton

Facts On File Publications
460 Park Avenue South
New York, N.Y. 10016

Copyright © 1984 Blandford Press Ltd

First published in the
United States by
Facts on File, Inc.
460 Park Avenue South
New York, N.Y. 10016

Library of Congress Cataloguing in Publication Data

Wootton, Anthony.
  Insects of the world.
  Includes index.
  1. Insects. I. Title.
QL463.W876 1984 595.7 83-25425
ISBN 0-87196-991-2

Typeset by August Filmsetting, Lancs
Printed in Hong Kong by Lee-Fung Asco Printers

Contents

Picture Credits

Preface

It is curious to reflect, as we stand on the threshold of interplanetary exploration and speculate about the possibility of life forms on other planets, that we are still lamentably ignorant about the most numerous and – arguably – important class of animals on earth. Insects comprise well over three-quarters of all the world's living creatures – and that is to consider only those 800 000 or so that have been catalogued and given names, for the plain fact is that no-one has even the remotest idea of how many species of insects there are in existence, except that the figure almost certainly runs into several millions. Even the life history and general habits of a great many 'known' species have been only sketchily studied, and in some cases they have not been studied at all.

All this may strike readers new to entomology as rather strange since, as everyone knows, insects tend to be extremely intrusive on our lives. They eat our crops, sting or take samples of our blood, assume squatters' rights in our houses, or even – as in the case of the fearsome driver or army ants – actually put us to flight. The fact is, though, that while some insects force their attentions upon us in this way, the vast majority are far more secretive and retiring and scarcely bother us at all. Myriads of them live in remote areas, which have been only sparsely explored by man (especially in regard to insects), or are very small and easily overlooked. In fact, one reason for the insects' staggering success as a group lies in their limited size and consequent ability to exist in all parts of the world and in almost every conceivable type of habitat. They occur from the arctic tundra to steamy jungles, from arid deserts to homely, grassy meadows; hosts of them live in wood or waste materials, in water or other liquids; and, taking the class as a whole, they can feed on just about anything, as well as breed at a truly astonishing rate.

Just about the only major habitat the insects have *not* yet managed to conquer is the sea and, even here, some species have made tentative steps towards so doing. Will they, one wonders, add these great turbulent wastes to their domain in a few million years? It is not beyond the bounds of possibility. After all, since insects have a far longer pedigree than man, there is absolutely no reason why they should not still be here long after *Homo sapiens* has finally become extinct or blown himself up. The post-holocaust insect is unlikely to be the man-sized ant of popular science fiction, but it will probably be able to develop strains resistant to atomic radiation, for there is no question that insects are quick to adapt to changing conditions and, indeed, are still evolving. Even now, some of them can tolerate the most extraordinary extremes: locust eggs can remain desiccated but still viable for several years and other insects are able to withstand temperatures way below zero by possessing a sort of anti-freeze in their blood.

Because some insects are troublesome to man, and so resistant to his efforts to control them, it is easy for the entomologist to adopt a somewhat defensive line and be reduced to offering excuses for their activities or even their very existence. I do not propose to do that because, for one thing, insects are of the greatest benefit to mankind – as plant pollinators, as scavengers and decomposers, as producers of essential products (such as honey and silk), as monitors of pollution and, indeed, as an essential part of natural ecosystems. It is no exaggeration to say that without insects the natural world would grind to a halt or would certainly be very different and by no means so pleasant. In any case, insects are attractive and interesting in their own right. Many of them, like butterflies, dragonflies and the magnificent jewel and diamond beetles, are quite as beautiful as any bird of paradise or humming-bird and their varied shapes, adaptations and behaviour patterns provide a never-ending source of fascination and delight. Needless to say, no one book could present more than a tithe of all this collective wonder, but I hope the present volume will at least provide some idea of what marvellous animals the insects are.

Anthony Wootton
Stone, 1983

Chapter 1

What is an Insect?

Non-entomologists in general, and popular newspapers in particular, tend to label any small, creeping, multi-legged invertebrate as an insect and are frequently somewhat mystified when it is pointed out to them that, say, a spider, centipede or woodlouse does not properly come into this category. Even so, the entomologist should not feel himself too superior in the matter, since trying to express a typical insect's basic characters in a few well chosen words, i.e. in terms that embrace the whole class, is virtually impossible without a liberal sprinkling of 'buts' and 'excepts'. In this, and in just about

This brilliant Peruvian butterfly (*Haemactis sanguinalis*) is a member of the skipper family (Hesperidae).

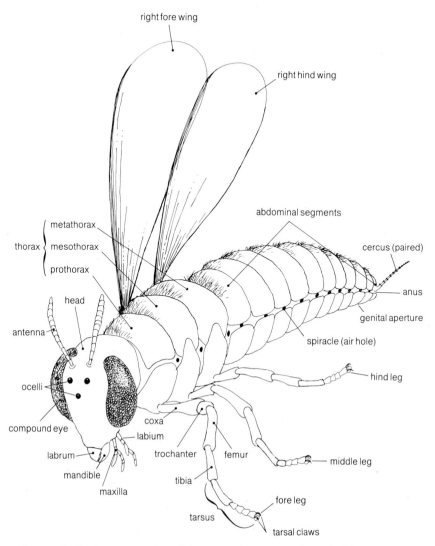

right fore wing

right hind wing

abdominal segments

metathorax

thorax { mesothorax

prothorax

head

antenna

ocelli

compound eye

labrum

mandible

maxilla

coxa

labium

trochanter

femur

tibia

tarsus

fore leg

tarsal claws

cercus (paired)

anus

genital aperture

spiracle (air hole)

hind leg

middle leg

Fig. 1.1. Stylised representation of the external structure of a typical insect.

every other particular, insects refuse to be placed into those neat clear-cut compartments which delight order-loving man, but consistently throw up exceptions to such rules as we apply to them.

The best that can be done is to indicate a number of general features (Figs 1.1 & 2) which together present a sort of basic guideline of differentiation from other groups. In the first place, all insects' bodies comprise a number of close-fitting and more or less fused segments which are generally shaped and differentiated into three main parts. These are:

(1) the *head*, bearing the eyes, antennae and mouthparts;
(2) the *thorax*, consisting of three segments, the *prothorax*, *mesothorax* and *metathorax*, to each of which is attached a pair of legs (a feature which is the

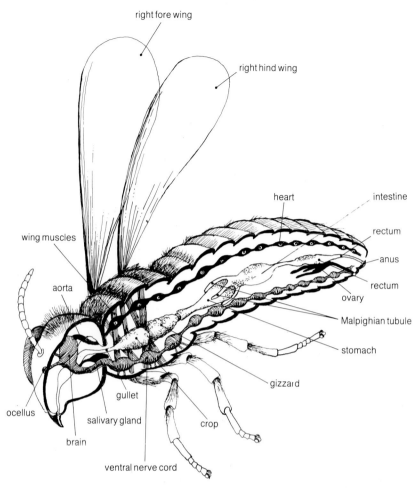

Fig. 1.2. Stylised representation of the internal structure of a typical insect.

basis of the alternative name, Hexapoda, of the whole group) and, often, on the last two segments, one or two pairs of wings;

(3) the *abdomen*, which may bear various appendages, such as *cerci*, mating claspers (in males) or (in females) an ovipositor or egg-laying device.

This is a useful basic guideline, but the problem is that there are a large number of insects in which the differentiation between head, thorax and abdomen is far from clear-cut (the primitive Apterygota are a prime example), while many insects lack eyes, a few (such as the Protura) have no antennae and there are a whole host of insects which either never possess wings or have them for only a short period of their lives, e.g. during courtship and mating. More importantly, such a definition entirely fails to take into account a bewildering variety of pre-adult forms (*larvae* or *nymphs*), whose bodies are often completely undifferentiated and either bear many more legs than six or, at the other extreme, none at all.

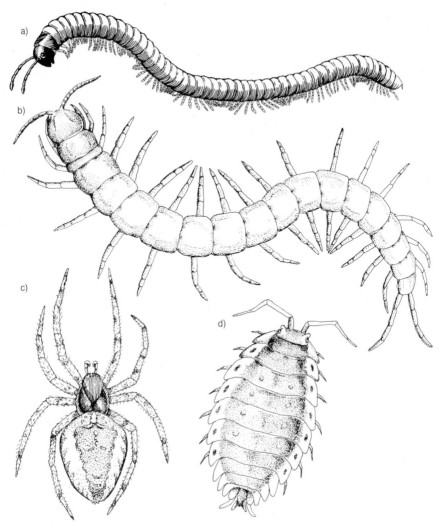

Fig. 1.3. Non-insect arthropods, showing their very different structure and leg numbers, etc. a) Millipede (Diplopoda). b) Centipede (Chilopoda). c) Spider (Arachnida). d) Woodlouse (Crustacea: Isopoda).

Faced with apparent contradictions like these, there is perhaps some excuse for the uninitiated's doubts about just what constitutes an insect and singles it out from other groups. After all, a beginner to the subject is just as likely to come across the multi-legged, wingless larva of a butterfly or sawfly as he is the progenitor of either. Moreover, close examination of a spider, centipede, millipede or woodlouse will reveal that they all share certain basic characters with insects (Fig. 1.3): an external skeleton (reversing the situation in vertebrate animals), consisting of an often *sclerotin*-toughened material called *chitin*, and legs which, while varying in number and

The magnificently coloured 'red skimmer' dragonfly (*Libellula saturata*) from Veracruz State, Mexico.

Army ants (*Eciton burchelli*) on the march in search of prey in a Trinidad rain forest. Colonies of army and driver ants frequently consist of many millions of individuals.

adaptations, are built on much the same general plan. In fact, it is shared features like these that prompt zoologists to classify all of these groups together in one great phylum, the Arthropoda (animals with jointed limbs and external skeletons), although each differs individually and is allocated to a separate class. Spiders and their allies, e.g. the scorpions, mites, ticks, false scorpions (class Arachnida), have the head and thorax fused to form a single section, called a *cephalothorax*; they have no antennae or wings and nearly always have four pairs of legs, even as young (mites sometimes have fewer). Centipedes (Chilopoda) and millipedes (Diplopoda) differ most essentially in the possession of a great many pairs of basically similar, clearly defined body segments, to most of which are attached one pair (centipedes) or two pairs (millipedes) of legs. Woodlice, the sole terrestrial relatives of the crabs and lobsters (Crustacea), have seven pairs of legs and a distinctive, variably curved, segmented body shield, called a *carapace*, which covers most of the body. There are other differences, both external and internal, but these are the most basic. Distinctions from other invertebrate animals, such as worms, are so obvious as to require no amplification.

Another feature that distinguishes insects from all other arthropods has already been referred to in passing: their method of growth. All arthropods hatch from eggs, either externally laid or developing within the female's body, but young spiders, centipedes, millipedes and woodlice are virtually miniatures of their parents. Insects, on the other hand, hatch from the eggs into larvae or nymphs, which commonly differ from the adult forms far more radically than in other arthropods, especially in those groups such as butterflies and moths, which undergo a complete metamorphosis, including a pupation stage.

Chapter 2
Origins of Insects

When animals are classified closely together the assumption is that they probably developed from a common ancestor at some remote time in their evolutionary history, and so it is with arthropods. Linked as they are by basic structural and physiological similarities, it is not unlikely that insects, spiders, centipedes, millipedes, symphylans and woodlice, together with their relatives, are all ultimately derived from some primitive worm-like creature, perhaps rather like the present-day marine polychaetes, but have diverged and developed into the different classes we know today, some remaining aquatic, others invading the land.

Just what this hypothetical arthropod ancestor was really like we can only surmise since the fossil record affords no clue to any direct line of descent, which might indicate successive changes into the forms we know today. We can only make educated guesses. Perhaps a rather later version was something like *Peripatus* (Fig. 2.1), a curious little animal which is so distinct that zoologists afford it a class status all to itself, the Onychophora. *Peripatus* is truly a living fossil, since it still exists today in Central and South America, Australasia and South Africa and yet remains of it, or closely similar forms, have been found in rocks as ancient as 500 million years. What is so fascinating about *Peripatus* is that it displays features that seem to put it halfway between the arthropods and the worms. It has arthropod-like antennae, primitive tracheae, or breathing passages, a flexible cuticle (worm-like except that it is dry) and some twenty pairs of fleshy legs like the pseudopodia of a caterpillar. It does not undergo any metamorphosis during its development and is also extremely dependent on a moist environment, which could indicate an aquatic origin. *Peripatus* is so like the larvae of some present-day insects, such as those of butterflies, moths and sawflies, that it prompts speculation as to whether such insects are recapitulating their evolutionary history via their development, a thesis more directly demonstrable in mammals, including man, whose embryo displays the vestiges of water-breathing gills and other non-mammalian characters.

Fig. 2.1. *Peripatus* (Onychophora): a 'living fossil'.

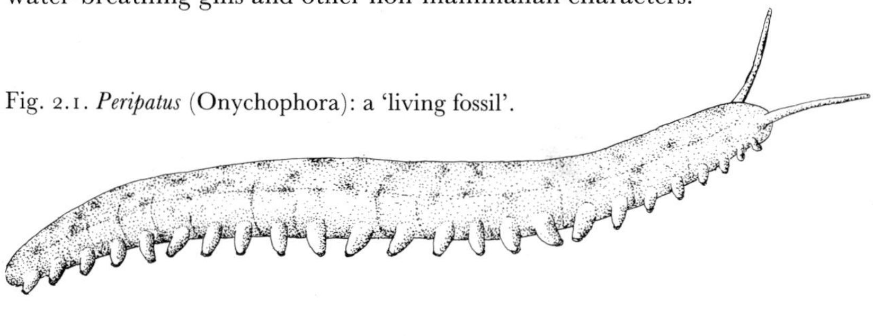

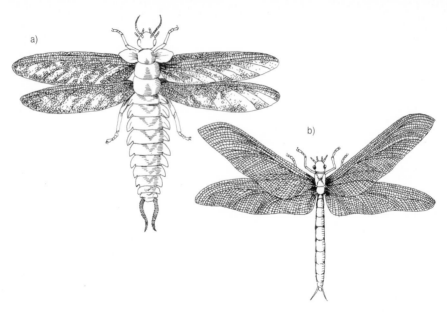

Fig. 2.2. Fossil insects. a) Reconstruction of an insect of the extinct order Palaeodictyoptera, showing the flap-like *paranota* on the first thoracic segment from which the true wings on the next two segments may have been derived. b) Dragonfly (Meganeura). Both are from the Carboniferous era, some 275–350 million years ago.

Unfortunately, there is no direct link between some *Peripatus*-like ancestor and fossil insects (Fig. 2.2). Indeed, the earliest insects are rather like Pallas-Athene who sprang fully formed from the head of her father Zeus – they arrive on the scene with no evidence of antecedents. The earliest known insect is a fossilised ancestral springtail (*Rhyniella praecursor*) from the Lower Devonian of Scotland, some 300–500 million years old. Nor are there any clues as to how and when the first winged insects came on the scene. These begin to appear in the Carboniferous, in the form of the primitive (now extinct) Palaeodictyoptera, closely followed by ancestral dragonflies, cockroaches and mayflies, some of them very large, with more advanced groups, such as the Hymenoptera and true flies (Diptera), appearing much later and the butterflies and moths last of all – in the Tertiary era.

Rhyniella and its fellows, while the oldest and most primitive of insects, are certainly not the ancestors of later winged forms, since springtails seem to have been always wingless and indeed, have come down to the present in that state, as well as virtually unchanged and distinct in other respects. What we can say, perhaps, is that they and the wingless Apterygota in general are probably nearer to the common ancestor of all insects. This contention seems to be borne out by the structure of these most primitive of all the insects, which display a variety of features linking them more closely with other arthropods. Springtails, for example, possess mouthparts closer in form to the Crustacea than other insects. Both Thysanura and Diplura (bristletails) display vestiges of legs additional to the usual six, while the latter's antennae are very like those of centipedes. The minute Protura lack antennae,

A common scavenger indoors, the silverfish (*Lepisma saccharina*) is among the most primitive of insects. It is a member of the order Thysanura – the three-pronged bristletails. England but cosmopolitan.

tenuously linking them with spiders, and also grow in a manner unique among insects, but typical of the crustaceans, by adding new segments in front of a structure called a *telson*, at the tail. The telson itself is found in no other insects, although it is a typical feature of the crabs, lobsters, and their allies, such as the terrestrial woodlice mentioned earlier.

Having said all that, it must again be emphasised that insect ancestry is extremely conjectural, since the evidence for it is either very fragmentary or non-existent. It is not impossible that there was no such thing as a common arthropod ancestor at all. It could equally well be argued that the various arthropod groups, and perhaps even some of the insect orders, have evolved quite independently on different occasions. After all, it is clear that, despite its limitations, the typical arthropod structure works exceedingly well and nature is not above repeating a successful experiment.

Chapter 3
Distribution of Insects

While insects occur throughout the world, and there are few orders without representatives in every continent, many regions have insect faunas which remain quite distinct from those of any other, even when the climate and terrain are similar. Thus, the tropical jungles of South America are the home of butterflies, such as Heliconiids, Morphos and Brassolids ('owls'), which occur nowhere else, as well as huge Dynastinid and Cerambycid beetles, brilliant, iridescent weevils, or 'diamond beetles' (*Entimus*), leaf-cutter or parasol ants (*Atta*), and a host of other forms. Indeed, it is probably true to say that the great continent of South America, together with Central America and the adjacent islands (e.g. Trinidad), can boast of a greater variety of insects than anywhere else in the world. However, that is not to say that other regions are not almost equally rich in species. Tropical Africa, for example, is the home of the great goliath beetles and also has some of the world's most magnificent butterflies, such as the great *Papilio antimachus*, with a wing span of some 230 mm (9 in). The incomparable birdwing butterflies (e.g. *Ornithoptera, Troides*) occur only in South-East Asia and New Guinea, where the intriguing leaf-insects (*Phyllium*) are also to be found.

Australia, too, has its distinctive insects, among them crow butterflies (*Euploea*), primitive stoneflies and ants, such as the aggressive *Myrmecia* (bulldog ants) and the only recently rediscovered *Nothomyrmecia*, widely believed to be the most primitive of all the living Formicidae. It can also boast of the largest living cockroach, *Macropanesthia rhinoceros*, which occurs in the Atherton plateau of north Queensland.

North America has a whole host of groups and species peculiar to itself, such as the periodical cicadas (*Magicicada*) and the weird-looking dobson-flies (*Corydalis*), yet, because of broad similarities in climate and terrain, and relatively recent geological isolation, its insect fauna in general displays many parallels with that of Europe and northern Asia. Eurasia itself offers much individuality, insect-wise, from one end to the other, although some butterflies and moths, such as the well known garden tiger (*Arctia caja*), occur from the British Isles in the west to Japan in the extreme east.

Continents naturally owe much of their individuality, as far as their fauna is concerned, to their isolation from other land masses and, even within a single continent, limitations of distribution may be effected by deserts, mountain ranges, and, of course, local climatic differences. Another factor influencing insects' range lies in their mobility. Many winged insects have

Leaf-cutter or parasol ants of the genus *Atta* carrying pieces of leaf back to their nest as a fungal mulch. *Atta* is Neotropical.

managed to establish a nearly worldwide distribution primarily through migration (Chapter 14), while others become virtually cosmopolitan through adaptation to human trading and their exploitation of man's dwellings and products. Such insect opportunists do not, however, affect the general pattern of insect distribution, which is systematised to some extent by the zoologist's arrangement of the world into a number of *zoogeographical regions* (Fig. 3.1), according to similarities in their faunal communities in general. These are:

(1) the *Holarctic*, which is further subdivided into (a) the *Palaearctic* (embracing Europe and the whole of northern Asia, including the Arctic, together with the African Sahara Desert) and (b) the *Nearctic* (North America and Greenland);

(2) the *Neotropics* (including the whole of South America north of Mexico);

(3) the *Ethiopian*, *Afro-Tropical* or *Sub-Saharan* region (Africa, south of the Sahara, including Madagascar and Southern Arabia);

(4) *Oriental* (including India, southern China, south to Thailand);

(5) the *Australo-Oriental* region (Malaysia, Indonesia, New Guinea, etc);

(6) the *Australasian* (Australia and Tasmania);

(7) the *Polynesian* (the Pacific Islands east of New Guinea, plus New Zealand);

(8) the *Antarctic*.

(Variations on this division will be found in other books; for example (5) and

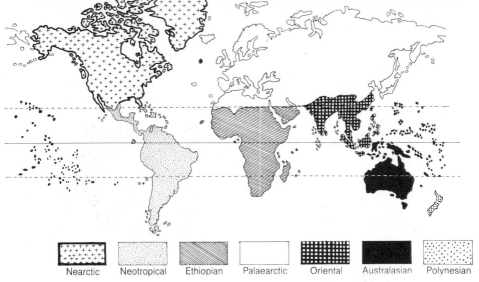

Nearctic Neotropical Ethiopian Palaearctic Oriental Australasian Polynesian

Fig. 3.1. The world's main zoögeographical regions. Their boundaries are far from precise, notably in the Pacific and in the area of overlap between South-East Asia and Australia, which is often referred to as a further (Australo-Oriental) region.

(6) are often treated as one region, primarily because they overlap so much in terms of animal species.)

Needless to say, the zoögeographical regions are not strict ecological units. Within each is found a variety of terrains (woodlands, grasslands, deserts, marsh, etc) supporting different insect faunas adapted to the particular conditions occurring in them.

Caterpillar of the birdwing butterfly (*Ornithoptera priamus euphorion*) of the family Papilionidae from a Queensland rain forest. Birdwings are peculiar to the Australo-Oriental region.

A cave-dwelling cricket (family Rhaphidophoridae) from Peru. This is a female nymph.

Insect life at the poles is naturally extremely scanty. A few hardy butterflies manage to penetrate the outer reaches of these areas but, for the most part, polar insects are confined to a few hardy wingless groups, such as springtails, or parasites of mammals and birds which counter the extreme cold by creating their own micro-climates amid fur or feathers. Quite a number of insects, however, manage to exist at the snow-line of high mountains, including the handsome apollo butterflies (*Parnassius*) and various 'browns' (*Erebia*), and the curious 'cricket-cockroaches' (Grylloblattodea) which only occur at high altitudes or in caves. Many cave-living insects, which include colourless, eyeless crickets and beetles, would appear to be relics of the Ice Age; initially retreating from the extreme cold, they have now become adapted to the still extremely chilly conditions below ground and are unable to exist outside. A number of these interesting survivals are found in cave systems stretching from France to Palestine, as well as in Virginia and Kentucky, USA.

Chapter 4

Anatomy and Movement

The idiosyncrasies of the typical arthropod structure and physiology militate against insects and their allies ever growing beyond a certain size. It is no accident that the very largest arthropods, such as spider crabs, are marine, since the water's buoyancy helps to counteract the animals' otherwise rather unwieldy, heavily armoured body. Insects, being basically terrestrial, are usually quite small, the vast majority of them falling within a size range of about 6–25 mm ($\frac{1}{4}$–1 in). There are a few relatively giant insects, but they tend to be sluggish movers and, significantly, are found almost solely in the tropics, where the warmth and humidity help to counter the problems presented by their size and weight. In fact, the very largest insects which exist today tend, for the most part, to be long and slim rather than uniformly bulky and there are very good reasons for this. Vertebrates can attain a much greater overall size since they have an efficient 'closed' means of rapidly circularising and energising all parts of the body via oxygen-transporting blood. Insects are not so equipped and are also far more dependent on external conditions for the degree of their activity than, say, mammals and birds. Insects' blood, which is a usually greenish liquid (called *haemolymph*) bathing the vital organs, plays little or no part in carrying oxygen or waste carbon dioxide but is concerned primarily with the transport of digested food and liquid waste, which is absorbed or exuded through the walls of the digestive tract. Instead, air for respiration is channelled into the body by means of a system of multi-branched tubes (*tracheae* and *tracheoles*) which open directly to the outer air through valved *spiracles* (Fig. 4.1). These are fringed with fine hairs to keep out extraneous matter and can be closed in adverse conditions. (The spiracles are especially recognisable on large, hairless caterpillars as small oval areas on the side of each body segment.) Such a system may sound efficient enough, but the problem is that air travels only slowly by simple conduction and its passage is slowed down still further in low temperatures when the air is denser. (This difficulty does not arise with the circulatory system of mammals and birds since oxygen readily combines with the haemoglobin in the rapidly-flowing plasma of their blood.) Consequently, oxidisation of food is a much slower business in insects than in vertebrates.

It is basically because of this that the majority of insects are small and narrow- or flat-bodied and have a thin cuticle, so that air does not have too far to travel. It is also probably why so many of them tend to be sluggish or inactive when the temperature falls below a certain optimum level, since their means of oxidising ingested food, to release energy, or even obtaining food in the first place, is considerably reduced. The giant-sized insects beloved of writers of science fiction simply could not exist for similar reasons. They would not merely succumb through their own weight but would also suffer from severe oxygen deficiency and quickly die for these reasons alone, even if they were not overcome by enemies.

Apart from imposing restrictions of size, however, it is abundantly evident, from the sheer numbers of insects, that their structure works remarkably well. An outer *cuticle* (Fig. 4.2), consisting primarily of a substance called chitin, variably hardened (more especially in adult insects) by impregnation with proteinous sclerotin, acts as protection from enemies, extremes of temperature and, more especially, water loss. Dehydration is, in fact, one of the insects' greatest problems, partly because of the thinness of the cuticle. The difficulty, however, is partly countered by the fact that most insects are able to secrete, in their epidermis, varying quantities of wax which forms a thin layer over the cuticle, which is both waterproof and reduces evaporation. Such a coating also helps aquatic insects to exist under water by preventing water from flooding their body tissues and may also prevent the drowning of any terrestrial insects that have had the misfortune to fall into water. It is extremely difficult to drown most insects since their shell-like structure makes them buoyant, while water simply slides off their surface or collects on it in small, rapidly dispersing globules.

Fig. 4.1. Insect respiration. a) Air is initially taken in via the spiracles and transported along a ramifying system of tracheae and tracheoles. b) Simplified diagrammatic representation of the insect respiratory system.

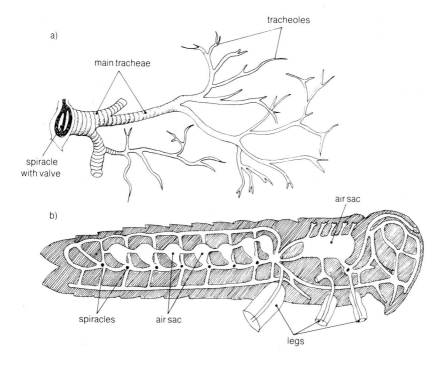

A huge goliath beetle (*Goliathus druryi*) from the Kakamega Forest, Kenya.

Fig. 4.2. The insect cuticle.

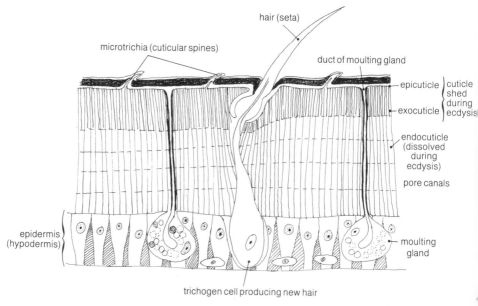

hair (seta)

microtrichia (cuticular spines)

duct of moulting gland

epicuticle } cuticle shed during ecdysis

exocuticle }

endocuticle (dissolved during ecdysis)

pore canals

epidermis (hypodermis)

moulting gland

trichogen cell producing new hair

26

Some moths, like this *Argema maenas* silk-moth, hanging from a tree-fern in Malaysia, attain a large size.

If the outer skeleton dictates an upper size limit, it also involves certain difficulties, or rather peculiarities, in growth. Since an insect's cuticle is composed of a non-living substance, its possessor cannot increase its size by simple cell division, as in the vertebrates, but has to shed its 'skin' whole. An insect's development from egg to adult (*metamorphosis*) is discussed in Chapter 8), but it is perhaps worth mentioning here that such a method of growth is not quite so cumbersome and 'painful' as it may appear to someone watching, say, a dragonfly emerging from the fully grown nymph. The larval or nymphal cuticle is, in the main, less sclerotised or hardened than

In this Saturnid moth caterpillar (*Dirphia molippa*) from Trinidad, the spiracles can be seen as white ovals outlined with black along its sides.

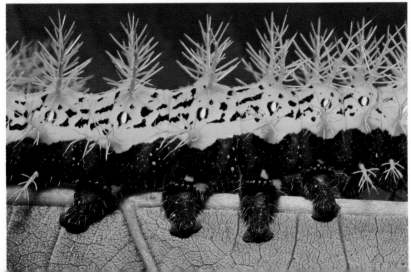

that of the final adult form and thus can be sloughed off rather more readily. In winged insects, moreover, wings do not appear until the final adult emerges and, initially, they are soft bag-like tissues which only attain their rigidity after being distended with blood or air.

As will be seen later, insects are well equipped sensorily to react quickly to external circumstances. Their vision, primarily the function of a pair of large compound eyes, may not be as efficient as that of mammals and birds, but their other senses, particularly those of smell and taste, are often exceedingly acute. Stimuli are received and actions initiated by a brain, which extends into a series of ganglia, forming the ventral nerve cord. Each ganglion tends to control the actions of that part of the body nearest to it, e.g. those in the thorax dictate the movements of the legs and (if present) wings.

Limbs and Locomotion

An insect's legs, the exocuticle of which (like the 'skeleton' proper) is shed during ecdysis, consist of a series of segments which articulate with the body and each other principally on a ball-and-socket basis. Muscles running through their hollow length allow only limited direction of movement, just as in vertebrates. The principal parts of the legs bear names similar to those applied to the vertebrate limb (Fig. 4.3). The largest and strongest is the *femur*, which articulates with the *tibia*, which in turn articulates with a usually segmented *tarsus*, commonly equipped with claws and pads (*pulvilli* and *arolia*) for gripping various surfaces. The femur, which may be considered analogous to the human thigh bone, is linked to the body by means of two smaller sections, the *coxa* and *trochanter*, whose length varies according to their owner's mode of life. Indeed, while this general plan is followed by most insects, the structure of the legs varies enormously from one group to another (Fig. 4.4) and often individually. Grasshoppers, flea-beetles, fleas and froghoppers, for example, have hind femora greatly enlarged for jumping purposes, contrasting with mantids and certain predatory bugs (Heteroptera) whose forelegs are strengthened, elongated

Fig. 4.3. Generalised limb of an insect.

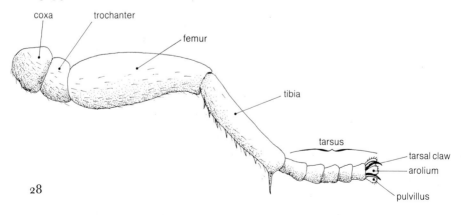

and barbed for securing prey. Aquatic insects commonly have one or more pairs of their legs enlarged and thickly fringed with hairs to aid in swimming. A particularly extreme example of leg specialisation is displayed by mole-crickets (*Gryllotalpa*), whose forelimbs are greatly enlarged and flattened,

Fig. 4.4. Specialised limbs. a) Diving beetle (*Dytiscus*): hind leg fringed with swimming hairs. b) Whirligig beetle (*Gyrinus*): middle and hind legs with bunches of bristles for surface swimming. c) Honey-bee (*Apis mellifera*): pollen basket (corbicula) on tibia of hind leg. d) Praying mantis (Mantodea): forelimbs modified for seizing prey. e) Dor-beetle (*Geotrupes*): tibiae of forelegs serrated for digging. f) Mole-cricket (*Gryllotalpa*): forelimbs adapted for digging and cutting roots. g) Grasshopper (Acrididae): hind femora specially adapted for leaping.

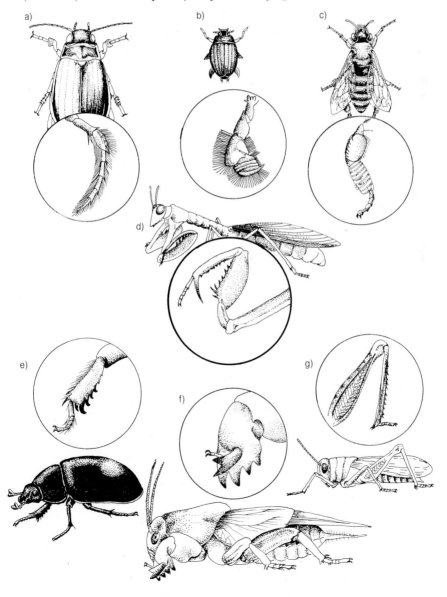

Grasshoppers, crickets and bush-crickets are able to jump by means of enlarged hind legs. This male *Agriacris trilineata* from Peru is raising its strongly barbed hind legs in a defensive attitude.

with the tarsi in the form of cutting shears for digging through soil and cutting roots; the other two pairs of legs are not so specialised. In some cases, an insect's legs are so weak as to be virtually useless for ordinary locomotion, as in the short-lived mayflies and also in the craneflies, which lose their legs with almost cavalier readiness.

The legs of the majority of terrestrial insects tend to be undifferentiated and much the same size, adapted for walking or running. Walking in adult insects is usually effected by alternate movements of the legs, two on one side (the first and third) being in the air while the corresponding pair on the other side are on the ground (Fig. 4.5). The overall effect is thus to propel the insect forward by a constantly alternating tripodal movement, the legs in contact with the ground acting as levers. Forward progress is not entirely direct, of course, since the push afforded by the two legs on one side (as against the one on the other) inevitably directs the walker somewhat obliquely, but this is immediately compensated for by the next leg movement, which takes the insect in the opposite direction. The overall effect is of a zig-zag movement, with the walker seemingly undecided about its objective. Running in insects is essentially the same method as walking speeded up. Particularly fast runners, such as ground-beetles and cock-roaches, have rather longer legs than average which lift the insects higher off the ground, thus enabling them to increase their speed. In insects such as these, the basal leg joints (coxae and trochanters) may be strengthened to add mobility, while the terminal tarsal structure of the foot may be simplified so as to reduce contact with the ground. In other insects, more especially Dipterid flies, the ends of the feet are armed with cushion-like structures

Fig. 4.5. Walking/running beetle.

covered with tiny hairs, which act adhesively and are commonly effective for gaining a purchase on the smoothest surface. This is presumably at least partly why a house-fly, for example, is able to walk so freely over the ceiling, defying gravity!

Locomotion in juvenile (immature) insects varies considerably. In Exopterygote insects, i.e. those which do not pass through a complete metamorphosis, the nymphs possess three pairs of legs like the adults and thus progress in a basically similar manner. The Endopterygote larvae, on the other hand, frequently have a number of additional legs, or pseudopodia, which are nevertheless lost during the final transformation to adult, while

A typical butterfly or moth caterpillar has, in addition to the six true legs behind the head, four pairs of false legs or pseudopodia and a pair of hind claspers. This is the caterpillar of the death's head hawk-moth (*Acherontia atropos*). Europe.

Looper moth caterpillars, like this brindled beauty (*Lycia hirtaria*), have only two pairs of false legs and walk in a characteristic loop. Europe.

others, such as fly larvae, have none at all. Both conditions, as well as the many variations upon them, involve quite different methods of locomotion.

Caterpillars of butterflies and moths, as well as the larvae of sawflies, have from five to eight pairs of *false legs*, or *pseudopodia*, which move forward in a continuous rippling motion by means of the contraction and relaxation of vertical and longitudinal muscles. The larva, by means of these fleshy and often bristly pseudopodia, can cling to its food plant most effectively, the legs sometimes almost encircling a twig, making physical removal virtually impossible without inflicting irreparable damage. In some moth larvae, notably those of the Geometridae and some Noctuidae, this tenacity has evolved to such a degree that it seems to have taken precedence over walking. In these, the caterpillar's pseudopodia are reduced to just two pairs of hind claspers, admirably suited not merely for securing a firm hold on a twig or leaf but also for adopting the twig-like stance which enables most of the group to avoid detection by sharp-eyed birds. Locomotion in caterpillars of this type is distinctive and, to some extent, rather laborious. The initial movement is by the six true legs just behind the head: these secure a hold, while the hind claspers are drawn up close behind them, thus forming the caterpillar's body into a loop, not unlike the Greek letter Ω. Because of this characteristic mode of locomotion, caterpillars such as these are given such colloquial names as 'loopers', 'inch-worms' and 'measuring worms'.

Other insects lack anything like a series of pseudopodia but have a sucker-like structure (*pygopodium*) at the end of the abdomen that plays some part in locomotion, more especially when the body is relatively long, in which instance the true legs behind the head would merely drag the body along if it were not for such terminal assistance. Larvae of lacewings, Lampyrid beetles and Simulid and Acrocerid flies all walk in a looper fashion, using their terminal suckers as steadiers, although the 'loop' appearance is generally less exaggerated than in Geometrid moth larvae.

Significantly, most of those insect larvae poorly equipped with limbs, or lacking them entirely, either live surrounded by or immersed in their food or pabulum (e.g. Muscid fly larvae), or are tended by a worker caste (bees and wasps). In others, there may be a simple steadying device at the tip of the abdomen which helps the larva secure its hold after having wriggled to another part of its pabulum. The wood-feeding larvae of horntails or wood-wasps (Siricidae) and root-consuming cranefly larvae or 'leatherjackets' (Tipulidae) are typical examples. Rather curiously, the caterpillars of some butterflies and moths have legs, both true and false, which are so reduced that they appear to play little or no part in locomotion; instead they seem to move by a combination of muscular contraction and the use of tiny suckers on the ventral surface. Among the most striking exponents of this type of locomotion are larvae of the peculiar slug-moths (Eucleidae), species of which display considerable variation in shape and colour pattern, as well as batteries of barbed spines for protection.

Wings and Flight

As we saw earlier, not all insects are capable of flight. Some, notably the primitive Apterygota, never possess wings and appear to have come down to us from the very earliest times in that condition. Others are secondarily wingless and either possess wings for only a short time and for a specific purpose, e.g. courtship and mating, or have lost them at some stage in their evolutionary history. Queen ants, which bite or rub off their wings after mating, are a typical example of the former, while ant workers, fleas, lice and many flies, beetles and bugs are among those insects whose life style is such as to render flight unnecessary and wings an actual disadvantage. Winglessness may also be an essential ingredient of *sexual dimorphism* and, where this happens, one or other of the sexes (usually the female) is incapable of flight and merely waits for the male to visit her. There are even some insects which

A wingless predatory damsel-bug (*Dolichonabis limbatus*). The forelegs are adapted for seizing insect prey. Europe.

possess fully developed wings but because of fairly recently adopted terrestrial habits rarely use them. The common earwig (*Forficula auricularia*) is a prime example and is probably a case of regressive evolution.

Despite these exceptions, flight is a typical insect feature and, moreover, of a character unique to them. Unlike the far more recently evolved wings of birds and bats, insects' wings are not specially adapted limbs but separate outgrowths quite distinct from the legs. There may be one pair, or more usually two, attached to the second and third thoracic segments and they are operated by special sets of muscles which direct their vertical movement. In

Fig. 4.6. Range of wing shapes and venation. a) Locust (Orthoptera). b) Dragonfly (Odonata). c) Cicada (Hemiptera: Homoptera). d) Alder-fly (Megaloptera). e) Stonefly (Plecoptera). f) Butterfly (Lepidoptera). g) Sawfly (Hymenoptera). h) are fast and effective fliers. Europe.

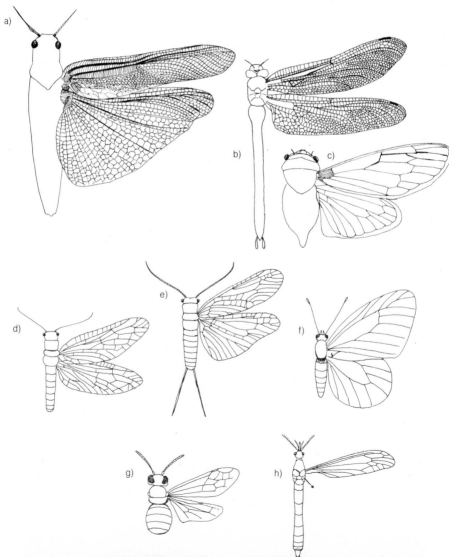

most insects with just one pair of operative wings, the hind pair are replaced by small peg-like structures called *halteres*. Essentially, an insect's wings consist of a double layer of chitin, exceedingly thin and interspersed with a supportive framework of hollow veins which are generally air-filled or charged with blood. Such venation varies considerably from group to group, and even from one species to another, and is thus an important guide to identification (Fig. 4.6). Mostly the wings are simply unembellished membranes, although they may frequently be highly coloured. In some groups, however, they are protected by a dense pattern of overlapping scales (butterflies and moths) or hairs (caddis-flies).

The most primitive insect fliers are generally considered to be those in which the two pairs of wings are both unlinked in flight, so that they flap independently, and are also incapable of being held at rest in more than one position. Of these, dragonflies are a typical example. Apart from a short period just after emergence from the fully grown nymph, dragonflies can only hold their wings fully extended in a lateral position when resting. Their flight, particularly hovering, is a flapping affair, each pair of wings working independently, the forewings creating a downbeat while the underwings beat upwards, and vice versa, the overall effect being of a rapidly changing X-shape. Such a flying technique suggests that dragonflies are capable of only limited speeds, but this is far from being the case. Partly because of their size and strength, dragonflies can attain very creditable speeds; some species of *Anax*, for example, have been reliably timed at 30 km/hr (18 mph). Although they have no means of linking the wings to work as a unit,

A male emperor dragonfly (*Anax imperator*). Despite their primitiveness, dragonflies are fast and effective fliers. Europe.

dragonflies can also glide, locking the four wings into an immovable whole by means of muscles in the thorax – commonly audible as a distinct click. Many other insects can do this and thus conserve energy, a considerable amount of which is expended in ordinary flight.

Other insects of ancient pedigree, such as mayflies, display far less efficient flight than dragonflies, while their wing musculature allows their wings to be held only in a vertical position when at rest. Most other four-winged insects have a much greater wing mobility. Moths, for example, can usually spread their wings laterally, vertically, or fold them down over the body when at rest, thus presenting a smaller target for enemies and also helping to conserve body heat. In some essentially four-winged insects, the forewings are not used for flight but have become adapted as protective covers for the operative underwings. The forewings (*tegmina*) of grasshoppers and phasmids protect underwings which open out like a fan, frequently beautifully coloured, while in other groups, such as beetles and earwigs, the wings may be tucked away beneath their covers (called *elytra* in these groups) in a most complicated, multi-folded fashion. In such insects, the protective covers are simply held out of the way of the wings proper during flight, whereas in those insects with two pairs of fully operative wings, both are commonly linked together so that they work in unison. Linking devices vary widely. In butterflies and some moths, the upper and lower wings perform as one because of an overlapping fold on the hind edge of the forewing, which thus pushes the hindwing with it on the down stroke. In others there is a more elaborate coupling device consisting of a spine, or *frenulum*, on one wing which is held by a catch or a group of bristles (*retinaculum*) on the other. Bees and wasps have an even more elaborate series of hooks and catches on their wing margins.

Many four-winged insects are among the supreme masters of insect flight. Hawk-moths, various butterflies, e.g. the powerfully flying *Charaxes*, as well as dragonflies, are capable not merely of remarkable bursts of speed, tacking backwards, hovering, and so forth, but of maintaining flight for quite astonishing lengths of time, especially during migration (see p. 167). However, it is probably safe to say that the peak of flying virtuosity has been attained by those insects which have reduced their motive power to a single pair of wings. These, for the most part, are the Diptera, or true flies. In this large group, which includes both superb aeronauts and completely flightless insects, the forewings have greatly reduced and refined venation, while the hindwings have been replaced by club-ended halteres, which seem to exert a kind of gyroscopic balancing effect in flight, raising and dipping according to the insect's position. One of the fascinations of this ultimate two-winged condition is that there is clear evidence (for once!) of a direct evolution from some four-winged fly ancestor. Laboratory experiments with fruit-flies (*Drosophila*) have occasionally resulted in the appearance of some individuals with two pairs of wings and others with half-formed underwings developed from the thoracic buds which usually become the halteres.

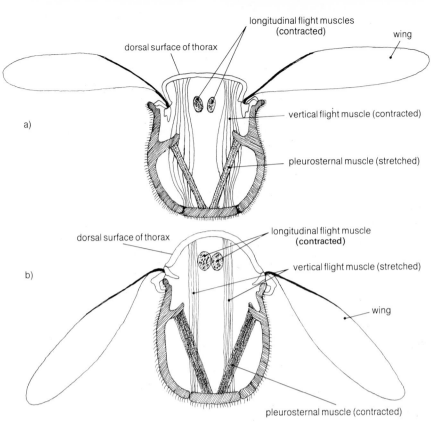

Fig. 4.7. The wing movement mechanism in advanced insects. a) During upward wing-beat, the longitudinal flight muscles expand (stretch) while the vertical flight muscles contract (shorten). This in turn induces stretching of the pleurosternal muscles and the forcing out of the thoracic wall, pushing the wings up out of their restraining catches. b) In the downbeat, the longitudinal flight muscles contract (shorten) and the vertical flight muscles expand (stretch), raising the dorsal surface of the thorax; the pleurosternal muscles contract (relax), pulling in the thoracic wall and the wings onto their catches and down.

Some true flies, particularly hover-flies (Syrphidae), are quite superb masters of flight control. A hover-fly can at one instant dart away at a speed almost too fast for the eye to follow and, at the next, hover with the body almost completely motionless and with wings that are a mere blur of movement. Such acrobatics involve much faster wing movements than are possible in other, four-winged, insects, whose flight mechanism is generally of a simpler kind. In groups such as dragonflies, mayflies, grasshoppers, cockroaches and beetles, the wings are moved by two sets of muscles directly attached to their bases: they work in harness and in opposition, alternately pulling the wings up and down by contraction and relaxation of each set of muscles. Flies, bees, moths and other more advanced fliers employing more rapid wing movements have, on the other hand, flight musculature which does not directly articulate with the wings at all but thrusts them up and down by alternately depressing and raising the upper surface of the thorax

Beetles raise their protective elytra (adapted forewings) while in flight. This cardinal beetle (*Pyrochroa serraticornis*) is just taking off from a buttercup. Europe.

that supports them (Fig. 4.7). These muscles are positioned at right angles to each other, one set being vertical (i.e. in the plane that a pin is placed in a set specimen) and the other longitudinal. They operate with such rapidity, aided by the elasticity of the thorax which is impregnated with a rubber-like substance, called *resilin*, that a much faster sequence of wing beat is possible. Even greater frequency of wing beat is effected in some groups by fibrillar muscle, which contracts and relaxes with such near automatic and continuous rapidity, initiated by a single nervous impulse, that the wings are seen only as a mist of movement. In addition to this, brief surges of power may be achieved by the wings being momentarily held in their up or down position by tiny catches until the build up of tension causes them to be suddenly released. Changes of speed or direction are brought about by other sets of muscles.

The movement of an insect's wings is not just a simple up and down affair. Forward propulsion and upward movement are gained by oscillatory movements and changes of wing angle, creating variations in air pressure. The initial movement of an insect's forewing for example, involves the inclination of its leading edge (coxa) to produce an area of low pressure in front, into which the insect is propelled, as well as an area of higher pressure beneath, which provides lift. There is considerable wing stress during flight and, since most of it is taken by the leading edge of the forewing, this area tends to be strengthened and thickened with supportive veins behind.

First Fliers

Precisely how insects first conquered the problems of flight and evolved wings is shrouded in mystery. It is possible that simple gliding evolved when early insects, perhaps leaping or falling from a height to avoid predators, gradually began to develop extensions of the thorax which, by acting as simple parachutes, helped to reduce the impact of their fall and increase their chances of survival. Subsequently, we may assume, these projections increased in size and specialisation and developed musculature, leading to controlled flight. Once again, the fossil record is unhelpful in providing definite support for such a theory: certainly there is no series of increasingly efficient flying prototypes that would help us to trace the steps by which flight was accomplished. However, it is interesting to note that the earliest known winged insects, the long extinct Palaeodictyoptera or 'ancient cockroaches', possess not merely two pairs of operative wings but a pair of what seem to be aborted wings or 'halfwings' on the thoracic segment in front of them. Obviously, three pairs of wings would be clumsy in the extreme and probably inoperable as a flying unit, so it is not unlikely that insects' wings began as these flap-like extensions but that only those on the second and third segments of the thorax developed fully.

Whether we accept this theory or not, one thing is certain: insects are the undisputed pioneers of animal flight. They are also the only invertebrates to have developed wings. Long before even the first pterodactyl took to the air, huge dragonflies, some of them with a wing span of more than 600 mm (24 in) were zooming over the Carboniferous swamps that, some 300 million years ago, gave rise to our present-day coal measures. Other insects, such as mayflies, cockroaches, stoneflies and grasshoppers, whose flight technique remains relatively primitive, were either contemporary with them or not far behind as aerial pathfinders. The flies, butterflies and moths that came later brought with them a much improved mastery of flight and, while all of them have long been extinct, their descendants have survived virtually unchanged as the most specialised fliers on earth.

Insect monoplane. The wings of this hoverfly (*Syrphus balteatus*) are a mere blur as it prepares to land on a dandelion flower.

Chapter 5

Senses and Communication

An insect's perception of the world is very different from our own and the five senses to which we are accustomed – sight, smell, taste, touch and hearing – vary in their nature and importance among the different groups.

Eyes and Vision

It is often said that a person's eyes are the first feature we notice about him or her and the same may be said to apply to many insects, if for a subtly different reason. The most readily identifiable of their sense organs, insects' eyes are often extremely large, so much so as to take up the greater part of the head, particularly in such groups as flies and dragonflies. In others, they may be much smaller and in some, especially subterranean groups, they are completely absent. It follows from this, therefore, that insects' sight varies in importance from group to group, depending principally on habits. Predatory dragonflies, for example, have exceptionally large eyes, which are mounted on a freely swivelling head and are sensitive to the slightest movement – rendering these insects particularly difficult to approach closely and photograph.

It is, however, easy to be misled as to the efficiency of the insect eye and, to obtain a clearer idea of its functioning, it is useful to make a comparison with its human counterpart. The human eye consists of a single convex lens which can focus over a great range by means of attached muscles; working together, the two eyes produce an image on the retina which is interpreted by the brain as both sharp and three-dimensional. An insect's compound eyes are very different in both structure and performance. They are called 'compound' because they consist of a large number of facets, commonly hexagonal in shape, which together make up a mosaic pattern of a curved or semi-circular form, corresponding to the curvature of the insect's head (Fig. 5.1). Each facet, or *ommatidium*, consists of a thin outer cuticular layer, slightly biconvex in form, which acts as a simple, rigid lens though lacking muscular attachment or any means of altering its focal length. Light received by the lens is directed through a crystalline layer, or secondary lens, to a group of retinal cells at the base of the ommatidium which then pass the image or light message to the brain by means of optic nerve fibres. Each lens, with its corresponding light-conducting apparatus, functions as an individual unit, conical in shape, and is usually cut off from its fellows by a light-

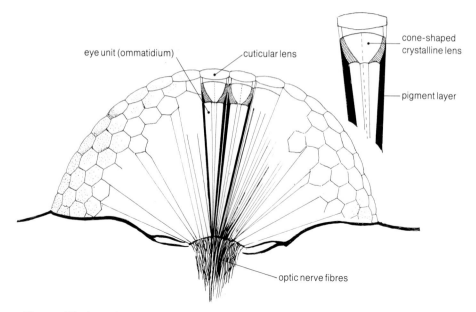

eye unit (ommatidium)   cuticular lens   cone-shaped crystalline lens

pigment layer

optic nerve fibres

Fig. 5.1. The insect's compound eye is composed of a large number of separate units (ommatidia). A single ommatidium is shown in the inset.

masking layer. From this, it is clear that any image received by the insect eye must be very different from that seen by man, mammals and birds, since the ommatidia work independently and pick up only that part of the viewed object which is immediately in front of them, as separate points of light, varying in intensity; since none of the lenses can focus, the overall effect must be extremely blurred and imperfect. Obviously, the image of what is seen by an insect gains in sharpness according to the number of facets in its eyes: the greater their number, the more precise the definition and the better the ability to interpret movement and changes in light intensity.

This is precisely why the dragonflies mentioned earlier are so difficult to surprise, since their eyes contain probably the greatest number of ommatidia of all insects – up to 30 000 or so. Predatory insects of this type often, in fact, possess eye facets of different sizes: some larger and more geared to interpret light, others smaller to aid recognition of prey or mates etc. Praying mantids have a group of much smaller ommatidia in the centres of their compound eyes which help them to determine a potential victim's position and shape with greater accuracy and may give them something approaching stereoscopic vision when the two eyes are used in conjunction. In this connection, a mantis will turn its free-swivelling head and follow the movements of its victim with its dark-centred eyes, often almost 'looking over its shoulder' for the purpose. Whirligig beetles (Gyrininae) and some mayflies (e.g. *Cleon*) possess eyes which are, in effect, divided into two sections, with larger or smaller eye facets. In mayflies, which usually mate at dusk, the larger facets may help the insects to see and navigate in poorer light, while the smaller ones probably give greater visual acuity.

41

Most adult insects have a number of simple eyes (ocelli) in addition to compound eyes. This *Cyclochila* cicada from a Queensland rain forest has a triangle of three ocelli between its widely spaced compound eyes.

We have no definite way of telling precisely how an insect interprets the light it sees but it seems clear that it is very different from our impression of it. Insects can see colours, for example, but it is most unlikely that they see them in the same way that we do. All that we can say is that they seem able to differentiate between certain colours, basically yellow, green, blue and ultra-violet, and even with these it is probable that the distinguishing factor is not so much colour as brightness and tone. Insects' ability to perceive ultra-violet light rays is of particular interest since it suggests that, while their eyes are incapable of interpreting light of longer wavelengths (the red end of the spectrum), they can distinguish the effects of light produced at shorter wavelengths than we can. Nectar-seeking bees and butterflies, for example, seem able to see flowers, not as the simple colours which we see but as a much more striking contrast of pale and dark areas. These are the honey-guides, leading to the flower's nectaries, darkly delineated since they emit ultra-violet invisible to the vertebrate eye. It seems clear that this ability to see in a different light, as it were, is usable by insects in various directions. Male Pierid butterflies, for example, may appear white to us but they also give off ultra-violet irradiations visible to the female butterfly; it is probable that white-winged ghost moths (*Hepialus humuli*), hovering low over grasslands in June and July, give off similar signals to the more richly coloured females waiting below.

The more we compare insects' eyes with those of vertebrates, the clearer it becomes that inferiority of performance in one direction tends to be compensated by superiority in another. We have already mentioned that insects can see further into the light spectrum (at least in one direction) than we can, and they are also able to see and interpret another kind of light that is beyond our capability. Day-flying insects use the position of the sun for orientation purposes and they tend to be thrown out of gear on cloudy days. However, as long as there are still one or two small patches of blue visible, insects can use these to tell the sun's position. They are, in fact, using *polarised light*, i.e. light which vibrates most strongly in one direction, leading from the sun. We are unable to interpret this plane of polarisation ourselves, but insects can and thus automatically compensate for their inability to see the sun directly. Many insects, such as honey-bees, do not even need patches of blue sky to determine the sun's position but use cloud-filtered polarised light, their eyes being especially sensitive to its quality and direction.

Bearing its limitations in mind, it is clear that the insect eye is not well designed for nocturnal vision. However, a variety of insects, especially moths, do seem to use the light emitted by the moon and stars as an aid to night navigation. Since the light rays from these bodies arrive from such a vast distance, they are to all intents and purposes parallel and, to fly on an even keel, a moth merely has to keep at the same visual angle with them; it is probable that it also uses them as fixed markers, compensating for their change of position according to season.

Obviously, nocturnal light navigation of this kind is also modified by other sensory stimuli, such as the scent of nectar-bearing flowers and potential sexual partners, but problems for night-flying insects arrive when they find themselves diverted by locally brighter artificial lights. Moths and other insects, such as beetles and caddis-flies, circling such a light source, are a familiar sight on hot summer evenings and it is a puzzle to many why they should be so irresistibly attracted. The answer seems to be that the insects have no choice in the matter. Initially they may try to navigate by means of such a light source but, since the light rays radiate in all directions, the insects vainly try to keep the same part of their eyes illuminated but end up spiralling into or around the light until they perhaps reel away totally bemused and blinded. One interesting feature of the eyes of nocturnal insects is that the pigmented layer that cuts off each ommatidium from its neighbours is either absent or capable of being concentrated into pockets, with the result that light 'leaks' from one segment to another. This obviously makes for greater light absorption by the eyes but, at the same time, must also cause dazzle when the insect is attracted to artificial light. It is this feature, too, which tends to make nocturnal insects' eyes glow like live coals.

Not all insect attraction to light is harmful. Indeed, in some groups, such as the fireflies and glow-worms, which belong principally to the beetle family Lampyridae, it is an integral part of their courtship. Here one or both of the sexes emits a kind of cold light as a signal or attraction to the other; in the European glow-worm (*Lampyris noctiluca*), for example, the winged male has very much larger eyes, geared for light perception, than the sedentary but more strongly luminescent female.

Compound eyes are not insects' only visual organs. Most insect larvae lack

Dragonflies have extremely large compound eyes made up of thousands of individual facets (ommatidia). This is a female southern aeshna (*Aeshna cyanea*) from the Severn Vale in Gloucestershire, England.

compound eyes but have groups of simple, single-celled eyes (*ocelli*) on the sides of the head; many adult insects also possess them commonly arranged in a triangle of three between the compound eyes. Basically they are of a similar structure to the ommatidia but seem primarily geared to appreciating different intensities of light, as distinct from vision proper. Nor is light perception invariably confined to eyes. In some insects, more especially

Acraea pentapolis pentapolis (family Acraeidae) from a Kenya rain forest. Butterflies have club-ended antennae whereas most moths' antennae are simple and thread-like or feather-like.

nocturnal or exceptionally light-shy groups, the surface of the body bears cuticular cells which are directly connected to light-sensitive nerve fibres. These in turn send electrically stimulated impulses to the brain and thus initiate movement away from the light source. Such a reaction occurs in domestic cockroaches and, significantly, may even take place when the more directly recognisable sense organs – eyes, antennae, cerci – are covered.

Role of the Antennae

The paired antennae that most insects bear on their head, usually between and slightly above the eyes, are commonly referred to as 'feelers', suggesting that touch is their primary role. In fact, their purpose varies considerably from one insect group to another, as do their size and shape. In insects such as dragonflies and damselflies, which rely principally on vision for locating food and mates, the antennae may be short and inconspicuous, whereas in others they may attain a very considerable length and are obviously of the greatest importance in the insects' activity. Long-horned beetles, bush-crickets and cockroaches possess exceedingly long thread-like antennae, sometimes very much longer than the body, which would seem primarily geared for sexual recognition. Worker ants are generally either very poor-sighted or quite blind and use their 'elbowed' antennae for mutual recognition purposes when they meet along foraging routes, passing their feelers caressingly over each other's heads. In situations like this, however, one cannot say that touch, pure and simple, is the only factor at work. The insects are almost certainly picking up subtle chemical emanations from their partners and are, in fact, not merely satisfying themselves of their shape but smelling and tasting them, too! This combination of antennal roles – olfactory and chemo-tactile – is typical of a great number of insects. Many insects use their specially modified antennae to locate food by its scent. Burying beetles (Silphidae), for example, have distinctive club-ended antennae, armed with numerous sensory hairs, that enable them to locate decomposing carcases from very considerable distances. Nectar-seekers may initially find their way to suitable flowers by scent, the antennae being naturally of particular importance to night-feeders, such as long-tongued hawk-moths.

Some of the most fascinating instances of the effectiveness of insects' antennae as chemo-receptors are displayed by moths. Male silk-moths (Saturnidae), tussock-moths (Lymantridae) and many others have elaborately branched or 'feathered' antennae which contrast strikingly with the far more modestly developed structures of the females. Here, the moths use their antennae as scent aerials, picking up the scent molecules of the females' *pheromones*, or 'love signals', from distances that may extend over several miles. What is interesting here is that the moths seem somehow able to distinguish between the females' subtle scent emanations – commonly unappreciable by the human nose – and the infinite number of other odours

A species of *Gnoma* from the New Guinea rain forest. Male members of the longhorn beetle family (Cerambycidae) commonly have very long antennae.

that must permeate the air on summer nights. Presumably, just as a wireless aerial can be tuned to pick up and distinguish between different sound wavelengths, a moth's antennae can distinguish between the different scents.

Some insects' antennae do in fact act as sound-wave receivers. Those of male midges and mosquitoes are quite as feather-like as moths' but are geared to respond to the sound of the females' wing beats, the whine of other males' flight, as well as that of other species, being ignored. While the antennae receive the sounds, interpretation of the latter is made by special

Ants commonly use their characteristically angled antennae for recognition purposes when two individuals meet. These army ants (*Eciton burchelli*) in the Peruvian rain forest are exchanging food.

46

Head-on view of a male puss moth (*Cerura vinula*) showing the branched antennae.

structures at their base called *Johnston's organs*. These organs are found on most adult winged insects, as well as in aquatic insects and larvae, although they may have varying sensory roles, such as assessing air velocity, water current and, notably in subterranean insects, the effects of gravity.

Many insects, especially larvae, have paired, usually filamentous, appendages at the end of the abdomen which probably play the part of anal antennae. These *cerci* are a special feature of soil-dwelling ground-beetle and rove-beetle larvae, for example, where it is an obvious advantage to have sensory receptors at the opposite end to the head. Nocturnal insects, such as crickets, have long tail filaments which probably play a tactile role, whereas those of mayflies, by contrast, may have more value as flight balancers.

Orthoptera – the crickets, bush-crickets and grasshoppers – have special 'ears' for receiving and interpreting the sounds made by other individuals of the same species. This Peruvian bush-cricket (*Stilpnochlora incisa*) has its tympana on its front tibia, just below the joint with the femur.

'Ears' and Hearing

Since a number of insects produce sounds quite deliberately, either as courtship signals or, less frequently, for defence, it is not surprising to find that they have quite elaborate hearing mechanisms, quite apart from the mosquitoes' antennae mentioned earlier. Crickets and grasshoppers, as well as cicadas, all produce sounds directly geared to attract the opposite sex and each has special membranes which vibrate in response, just like the *tympana* of the human ear. In crickets, the tympana are situated on the tibiae of the forelegs, which are commonly extended in the direction of the stridulatory sounds, whereas, in grasshoppers and cicadas, the drum-heads are positioned on the sides of the abdomen.

Insects like these are, of course, geared to receiving and interpreting just one type of sound but that does not mean that they are oblivious to other vibrations. Most insects have socketed hairs (sensory setae) scattered over much of the body which vibrate in response to sounds and may also be sensitive to touch, humidity and light. Nocturnal insects, such as cockroaches, are particularly sensitive to sounds via their setae and have been known to shy away from vibrations issued at 3000 cycles per second – way beyond human hearing capabilities.

The setae may also play other roles. Locusts use those on the head, between the antennae, to judge the direction and humidity of the breeze, and climb some eminence for this purpose. Subsequently, they may use the information thus gained to fly to areas of low pressure where rain is likely to induce lusher feeding pasture. The sense of touch, via the body hairs, is also an essential attribute of those insects which are strongly thigmotactic, i.e. exhibit a preference for shelters where as much of their body surface as possible is in contact with some moist, protective substrate. Such a trait is a feature of such insects as earwigs, as well as a variety of groups that shelter under stones and damp logs.

Appreciation of Time and Space

If insects possessed any real appreciation of time as we know it, which would obviously necessitate a brain of comparable size and complexity, then they would probably reflect, gloomily, on the transience of life. After all, the vast majority of them live only a few years at most (the greater part of that time as larvae) and some adults, such as mayflies, last but a few days or even hours. In one respect at least, however, they view the passage of time much as we do, in that they are able to divide up the day into periods of activity and rest, according to whether they are diurnally active or nocturnal. Naturally, much of this cycle of activity is clearly explicable in that it is linked to the variable hours of daylight and darkness, as well as temperature; but insects, like most animals, also seem able to regulate their activity quite independently of external influences by means of what may be called an internal or

A batch of eggs laid by a buff-tip moth (*Phalera bucephala*). Many insects lay their eggs in beautifully precise geometrical patterns.

physiological 'clock'. Precisely how this works is uncertain, although it appears that hormonal build-up is the prime factor in telling an insect when it should rest and when it should wake up. Thus it is that cockroaches, for example, become active at roughly the same time each day (or night) even when kept in continual darkness. Such a biological clock may also influence the time of the day when an insect emerges from the pupa (*eclosion*). This happens especially in those species with not very efficient means of controlling or regulating water loss; eclosion thus coincides with times, such as early evening and morning, when the air is moister and there is less chance of the newly emerged adult becoming dehydrated.

By some mysterious means, insects are also able to use the magnetic field and rotation of the earth, not merely as fixed points by which to navigate but also, presumably, to assess the passage of time as the position of north shifts according to the seasons. Insects can also learn and memorise. A sand-wasp (*Ammophila*), when returning to the vertical burrow which it has stocked with caterpillars for its larva, recognises its position from the stones and general configuration of the surrounding landscape; it becomes confused if these are changed but soon learns to adjust to the new arrangement. Bees and flies can be conditioned to respond to the promise of food, by extending their proboscides, when certain coloured lights are shone on them.

An ability to count, measure and design is another insect attribute. Ovipositing female butterflies seem able to count the number of eggs they deposit on leaves, spacing them out so that the emergent larvae do not have to compete for food. By contrast, many moths deposit their eggs in such neat, close-packed groups as would be difficult for any man-made machine to emulate. Case-making caddis larvae cut lengths of reed or leaf of precisely the right size, apparently by measuring them against the length of the forepart of their bodies. Bees and wasps instinctively construct cells of different size for workers, queens and males and, moreover, make them of a hexagonal shape which is geometrically the most efficient in terms of utilisation of space and materials.

Subjective Experience

One question that is often asked is whether insects experience pain or strong emotions. The question is difficult to answer since pain is very much a subjective sensation, even in human beings. Certainly, many insects have been observed to continue feeding with their abdomens severed, the imbibed nourishment simply issuing from the hind part of the thorax, which suggests that the sole effect of such mutilation is, eventually, to result in the feeders' death through starvation. Insects do, however, seem to feel distress when prevented from carrying out their normal activities. An incarcerated bee tends to panic as a result of hormonal and other chemical discharges into the blood and soon dies through nervous stress. Insects' defence of their young, especially human-like in lowly groups like earwigs and certain Heteropterid bugs (e.g. *Elasmucha grisea*, the parent-bug), seems clear evidence of affection in the insect world; but it can be explained in terms of *genetic altruism*: a means of giving the protected progeny a better start in life and therefore helping the perpetuation of the species. Certainly, a female earwig is exceedingly selfless in her devotion to her nymphs, rarely leaving them until they are capable of fending for themselves and starving herself in the meantime. Unfortunately she is but poorly repaid for her maternal love since it is quite common for the growing nymphs to eat her when she becomes sickly and dies. In insects' defence, however, it should be remembered that consumption of the recently departed, as well as cannibalism, was no uncommon thing in many human societies until quite recent times!

Chapter 6

Feeding, Digestion and Excretion

There is, as we saw earlier, really no such thing as a typical insect. All may share a basically similar structural plan, but individually they vary enormously and no more so than in their mouthparts which, in turn, give at least some indication of feeding habits and also identity. Nevertheless, to discuss the structural arrangement of insects' mouthparts, which differ greatly from those of a vertebrate animal, we need to begin with a model – a basically omnivorous or vegetarian insect whose mouthparts lack the extreme specialisation exhibited by other groups (Fig. 6.1).

Mouthparts

In predominantly plant-chewing insects, such as grasshoppers, the mouthparts consist primarily of a pair of sharp-edged, often serrated, biting or

Fig. 6.1. Simplified diagram of head and mouthparts of a typical herbivorous insect (e.g. grasshopper).

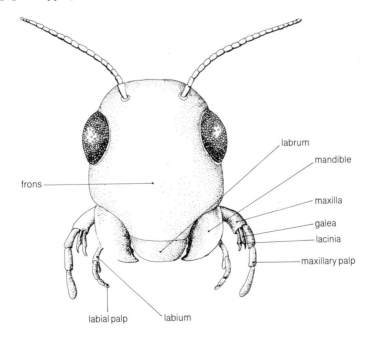

frons

labrum

mandible

maxilla

galea

lacinia

maxillary palp

labial palp   labium

cutting jaws (*mandibles*) which operate in a lateral direction, rather like hand-shears, to cut off pieces of plant. Behind the jaws are a pair of *maxillae*, which operate as secondary mandibles and bear at their tip a pair of structures, the *galea* and *lacinia*; the latter is often toothed and bristly to assist in holding and manipulating the food. Each maxilla also bears a jointed *palp*, as does an additional structure behind them, called the *labium* or 'lower lip'. The palps are at least partly sensory, the labials tasting and testing the plant material. Above and between the mandibles, as one looks at the insect's head face-on, is another structure hinged to the *frons* (face) called the *labrum*, or upper lip, which is primarily concerned with guiding the food between the jaws.

Such a system of mouthparts is typical of those insects which leisurely cut and chew their food. In other groups, individual parts are enlarged or adapted according to particular needs (Fig. 6.2). A flesh-eater, such as a ground-beetle, may have its mandibles greatly enlarged, pointed and barbed, for seizing and rending its prey. In others, notably bees, the mandibles may be retained but, as far as feeding is concerned, they are subordinate to an extension and modification of the upper lip (labrum) into tubelike *glossae*, adapted for sucking liquid nectar. A basically similar arrangement is found in the butterflies and moths, most of which have discarded their mandibles altogether; in their place is a hollow *proboscis* which in some species attains considerable length and, when not in use, is generally coiled up like a watchspring. The house-fly's sucking device is different again; it takes the form of an absorbent pad, the *haustellum*, through which digestive enzymes are poured onto the food (such as meat and sugar) before it is sucked up in liquid form through a connecting tube. In other insect suckers, such as bugs and fleas, the sucking device is of a piercing nature, the so-called *rostrum* being armed at the tip with minute serrations for cutting into the tissues of animals and plants before imbibing sap or blood, usually with the accompaniment of a digestive enzyme or anti-coagulant. In parasitic blood-suckers, like mosquitoes (see Chapter 7), all of the mouth-parts are adapted to support a pair of sucking stylets, working as one, the labium (lower lip), for example, forming a protective sheath which is slid up out of the way while the stylets do their work.

In some cases, an insect's mouthparts give a highly misleading impression of its feeding habits. Male stag beetles, for example, display grossly enlarged pronged mandibles which are quite useless for predatory or feeding purposes and are probably used mainly for sexual display or jostling with rival males. Insects like these can usually only lap liquid food or live on stored nutriments. Some adult insects do not feed at all and, consequently, have much reduced or aborted mouthparts. It is also worth pointing out that the feeding habits of adult and larval insects may differ considerably; adult ant-lions (Myrmeleontidae), for example, often content themselves with nectar as food, while their sickle-jawed larvae are predatory. Even when both adult and larva are predatory, methods of feeding and structure of the mouthparts

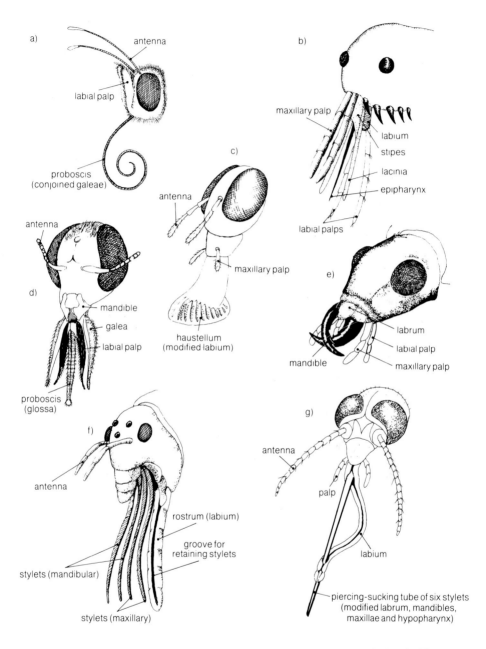

Fig. 6.2. Specialised mouthparts. a) Butterfly (Lepidoptera): nectar-feeder. b) Flea (Siphonaptera): blood-sucker. c) House-fly (Diptera): scavenger. d) Worker bee (Hymenoptera): nectar-feeder. e) Tiger-beetle (Coleoptera): predator. f) Aphid (Homoptera: Hemiptera): plant-juice sucker. g) Mosquito (Diptera): blood-sucker.

also tend to differ. Adult dragonflies have only moderately developed mandibles for capturing insect prey on the wing, whereas their aquatic nymphs secure their victims by impaling them on the terminal fangs of an extensible 'mask'.

Digestion and Excretion

The digestive system of an insect is simpler than that of vertebrates. Lacking such highly specialised organs as liver and kidneys, it consists for the most part of a tube, of variable thickness, running from one end of the body to the other and differentiated into three main parts:

(1) the *foregut*, comprising the oesophagus, or gullet, the crop and the gizzard;

(2) the *midgut*, containing the stomach;

(3) the *hindgut*, or intestine, which leads to the rectum and anus.

Food taken in by the mouth is partially digested by saliva and further broken down, by means of enzymes, in the crop, where it may also be stored for some time. It is then passed to the gizzard where any especially tough food is ground down into fine particles by means of its specially toughened and muscular lining. The food mass is then directed into the stomach, where the nutritive elements are extracted in liquid form and passed, through the stomach wall, into the sea of surrounding blood, where it is directly oxygenated by air brought in from the outside via the tracheal tubes. Solid waste is passed into the hind gut and eventually excreted, often in shapes characteristic of the insect. Liquid waste is dealt with by a bundle of *Malpighian tubules*, between the midgut and the hindgut, which perform a duty somewhat analogous to the kidneys in mammals. They extract excretory fluids from the blood and pass it back into the intestine, whence it proceeds for excretion with the solid material. In the larvae of groups which subsist primarily on liquids (e.g. Neuroptera), any solid waste material is accumulated in the system until the last ecdysis, when it is expelled together with the final cuticle. Some waste material also accumulates during the transformation from larva to adult and is only expelled when the latter emerges. Butterflies and moths, for example, commonly discharge a pinkish fluid soon after breaking out of the pupa.

Modifications of the digestive system take another form in those insects which consume only liquids and, in these, the gizzard may be reduced or absent; this may also be the case in those groups that partially digest their food externally – i.e. outside the body – by dribbling saliva upon it. Some groups, such as termites and beetle larvae, which consume wood or wood products have a large population of symbiotic micro-organisms in their hindgut which helps to break down the indigestible cellulose and convert it to sugars. Fleas and lice (Siphunculata) contain bacteria which are specially adapted for digesting blood and it is these micro-organisms which cause

Caterpillar of a copper underwing moth (*Amphipyra pyramidea*) feeding on willow leafage, together with the tiny nymph of a leafhopper bug which sucks stems and leaves instead of chewing them (like the caterpillar). England/Europe.

diseases in man and other animals when they are occasionally re-injected into the host's blood system.

Plant-Feeders

Among the characteristics which tend to give insects a poor public image is their apparent ability to consume just about everything in sight, more especially, or so it seems, cultivated plants. Accomplished opportunists as

Many bugs suck the sap of trees, like these Peruvian leaf-hoppers (*Proconia marmorata*) in rain forest.

they are, any intensified crop-planting is likely to be regarded by various insects as an open invitation to forestall the harvester and wreak devastation on foliage, flowers, fruits or even stems and roots. Even the humble back-gardener may be moved to wonder if his efforts are worthwhile when his brassicas are shredded by colonies of large white butterfly (*Pieris brassicae*) larvae, although such occurrences are as nothing compared to the devastation which can be caused by hordes of desert locusts or by such sucking bugs as the vine phylloxera (*Viteus vitifolii*), which has totally ruined the southern European grape harvest on more than one occasion, notably in the mid-nineteenth century.

Such unwelcome attentions prompt a somewhat one-eyed view of insect feeding activities, but the fact is that very few plants, cultivated or wild, escape the insects' attention and most of their food is comprised of species which are outside the grower's interests. Moreover, apart from seedling plants and those whose foliage is required for human consumption, well established plant growths generally suffer little from the effects of insect defoliators, however numerous they may be. Oaks, for example, have their foliage, flowers, shoots, roots and even bark and wood attacked by some hundreds of different insects, among them moth larvae and gall-wasps, but seem to grow ever the sturdier for it. In Britain, shrubs such as sallows play host to around 140 species of moth larvae, in addition to aphids, froghoppers, sawfly larvae and many others, yet still flourish. When insects do kill plants, it is usually because they inadvertently bring with them viruses or fungal spores which spread through and destroy the organism's system, as is the case with Dutch elm disease, conveyed by several species of bark-beetle (Scolytidae).

Of course, it is unlikely that all of the species mentioned as feeding on such trees as oaks and sallows will be found on one plant, (how marvellous for the lepidopterist if they were!), yet this is partly balanced by the communal feeding nature of many of them. Many moth larvae, such as the bristly yellow and black caterpillars of the buff-tip (*Phalera bucephala*), feed side by side in companies of perhaps a dozen or more, attaining a full size of nearly 50 mm (2 in). Lepidopterous larvae consume foliage in various ways. Some systematically shear off pieces from a leaf's edge, perhaps chewing down a certain distance and then recommencing at the top; others, smaller or younger, merely nibble at its surface; still others, notably the larvae of Nepticulid and Gracillariid moths, are small enough to feed between the upper and lower surface of a leaf, producing 'mine' effects which are often characteristic of the species that made them. Many other insect larvae produce feeding mines in leaves, both on trees, such as oaks, apple and holly, as well as on lowly dandelions and docks. They include tiny weevils and larvae of various flies, especially those of the family Agromyzidae. Suckers, rather than chewers, of foliage also tend to leave diagnostic feeding signs. Tiny lacebugs (Tingidae) produce a stippled surface on leaves which often reflects the minutely pitted surface and reticulation of their body and wings in a remarkable way and may well constitute a form of cryptic camouflage.

The champion plant-suckers of the insect world must surely be the aphids, of which there are many hundreds of species: 500 of them occur in Britain alone. Commonly, these communally feeding bugs will be found clustered about the stems of various plants since it is here that the plants' sap is under continuous flow and under such high pressure that all the insects have to do is pierce and imbibe with the minimum of sucking. Fleshier plant stems and leaves are particularly favoured by aphids but even more woody growths are not ignored. The lower stems of willows, for example, are likely to support colonies of the attractive *Pterocomma salicis*, coloured bluish grey with white spots and bright orange legs, antennae and siphunculi – tube-like structures from which the aphids can exude a repellent wax. Other sap-sucking bugs are solitary feeders. Froghoppers, which, considering their size, are as prodigious leapers as any grasshopper, feed openly as adults but as nymphs do so within an excretory protective froth which prompts the popular name 'cuckoo-spit'.

In the scale-insects, which are also members of the Homoptera, the older nymphs and also the totally sedentary females commonly feed beneath a waxy covering but the younger nymphs are more active; the short-lived males, which possess only one pair of wings, do not feed at all, having only vestigial mouthparts. Cicadas possess the ability to feed and 'call' at the same time – not surprisingly, really, since their song emanates from two membranes or *tymbals* at the sides of the body and is very far from being a voice in the mammalian or bird sense. The nymphs of the cicadas are also plant-suckers but feed on subterranean roots and often require several years to attain maturity.

Other, non-sucking, root-feeding insects have specially toughened, sclerotised jaws which enable them to tackle roots, bulbs and tubers. The wireworm larvae of click-beetles (Elateridae), with a hardened cuticle resistant to crushing, and the large fleshy larvae of chafer beetles are among the more notorious underground browsers. Other chafer larvae, such as those of the Central African goliath beetle, feed on decomposing wood, as do beetle larvae of the longicorn group and such species as the death-watch (*Xestobium rufovillosum*), whose tunnellings have ruined the superstructure of many a church, as well as the roof of London's twelfth century Westminster Hall. Wood-wasps, or horntails, not closely related to the social wasps, are another group whose larvae feed within the trunks of sickly trees or felled trunks and there are also a number of rather primitive moths with similar feeding habits. The peculiar caterpillar of the goat moth (*Cossus cossus*), dull yellow and livid red like a blood-blistered finger, burrows in the boles of sickly willows, exuding a characteristic goatlike smell.

It is perhaps not without significance that most larvae living in wood require several years to attain maturity. Wood is by no means a nutritious diet and, even then, most wood-feeders cannot manage without the help of a healthy population of cellulose-digesting protozoans or other organisms in their gut. Also many such larvae can only survive in their woody home if fungi have begun to weaken and soften it first. Ambrosia-beetles actually feed on the fungi that grow in their feeding tunnels in bark and wood.

We have mentioned elsewhere that certain ants and termites appear to deliberately cultivate fungi in their nests for consumption by adults and larvae. Free-growing mushrooms and toadstools also form the feeding home of a variety of insects. Mycetophilid fly larvae are particularly common inhabitants and may sometimes be a pest of cultivated mushroom beds. Adult and larval rove-beetles (Staphylinidae) feed on cap and stem when they are in the process of decomposing. Another kind of fungus food is provided by the near-liquid, spore-bearing caps of the stinkhorn fungus, which emits a peculiar foetid odour attractive to flies such as bluebottles, greenbottles and flesh-flies. So delicious do the insects find the liquid that it is generally consumed within an hour of the fungus's ripening. Nor is the bargain one-sided since the flies carry away some of the fungal spores on their body or pass some out with their faeces, thus assisting in the stinkhorn's spread.

Insects' overwhelming predilection for the nectar of plants, incidentally resulting in the latter's cross-fertilisation, is of particular interest since there is evidence to suggest that the two groups – insects and flowering plants – evolved in tandem at about the same time in pre-history. It is surely no accident that, just when the non-flowering, spore-producing ferns and cycads were undergoing a decline, to be replaced by plants bearing pollen and nectar, the insects, too, should undergo their own great 'flowering' of species. Clearly, the pattern of interdependence between the two was set very early on: the insects gaining a plentiful supply of sugar-rich nectar in return for (inadvertently) taking some of the flowers' pollen to others of the same species.

It is probable that, in the early days of flower development, insects were attracted to blossoms primarily by scent and colour, just as they are today. Other flowers, however, have evolved more elaborate means of gaining insects' assistance. Many orchids, for example, have evolved elaborate flower shapes which would seem to imitate bees, wasps and flies, both in appearance and scent, in order to deceive these insects into thinking them potential partners. The duped insect settles on the flower, attempts to mate with it and receives clusters of pollen grains (*pollinia*) which it is quite likely to transfer to subsequently visited flowers. Many flowers bear lines on their petals, leading to a contrastingly coloured centre, and these appear to direct pollinating insects to the nectaries at their base. So dusted with pollen do many insects become, especially bumble bees, that one would think that there was a constant danger of flowers fertilising themselves with their own pollen, but most species have devised elaborate means of preventing this either by the arrangement of the male anthers and female stigmas or by the male and female parts ripening at different times.

A wide variety of insects take advantage of flower nectar, among them

Some butterflies are able to feed on pollen, which they dissolve by means of special enzymes, then suck up in liquid form. They include the Neotropical Heliconiids, like this *Heliconius isabella* from Trinidad.

beetles, moths, butterflies and hoverflies, in addition to bees, but not all flowers offer access to it indiscriminately. The corollas of such flowers as *Nicotiana*, for instance, can only be negotiated by unusually long-tongued insects such as hawk-moths, among them the European convolvulus hawk (*Herse convolvuli*). In some South American Sphingids, the proboscis reaches a quite astonishing length, several times the length of the body and way beyond that necessary for feeding purposes.

Pollen is a nutritive food and is eaten by many insects. Many social and semi-social bees have means of actually transporting it back to the nest in considerable quantities, stroking it off the body with the forelegs into special bristly-edged *pollen baskets* on the hind pair. Mixed with honey, it is fed to the bee larvae. Butterflies generally have no use for pollen since they take only liquids, although some are known to consume small quantities by externally digesting it with exuded saliva. Tiny Micropterigid moths, among the most primitive of the Lepidoptera, untypically have chewing mandibles adapted for pollen consumption.

Harvester ants collect seeds and store them in special nest chambers for future consumption (see p. 128). Some smaller insects actually live within grain and other fruits and complete their larval development there. Grain weevils (*Sitophilus granarius*) lay their eggs within stored cultivated grains and can cause considerable problems to farmers. Often their activities are closely followed by mealworm larvae (*Tenebrio*), commonly used as pet food, which feed on the starchy flour spilled from the broken grains. Larvae of codling moths (*Cydia pomonella*) feed in apples, both wild crabs and cultivated. Gorse weevils (*Apion ulicis*) consume the beans within gorse pods and are forcibly expelled as adults when the casings dehisce. So successful are these little beetles in reducing the seeding viability of gorse that they have been exported to countries such as New Zealand to control the spread of the shrub. One of the most popularly fascinating insect seed-eaters is to be found in the famous jumping-bean, commonly sold as a novelty pet. The instigator

59

of the jump, often stimulated by the heat of the hand, is the larva of a tiny undistinguished-looking 'micro' moth, *Carpocapsa saltitans*, a native of Mexico, which lives within the woody seeds of *Sebastiana pavoniana* (milk-weed). Normally the jump, effected by convulsive movements, enables the imprisoned larva to avoid the heat of the sun when the seed is expelled by the host plant.

Predators

As exponents of biological pest control well know, some of the most effective reducers of plant-eating insects are other (predatory) insects. On the ground, in water and in the air, these carnivorous species wage a continual round of slaughter on their herbivorous counterparts, using methods and weapons which vary enormously, even from adult to larva. Sickle-jawed tiger-beetles (Cicindelinae), for example, are classic examples of the extrovert hunting type. Active in bright sunshine, typically on sandy heathland, with large protruding eyes denoting keen vision, they use their long legs, aided by short bursts of flight, to literally run down their victims, which may include other beetles, grasshoppers and a variety of other insects. By contrast, the tiger-beetle's equally predatory larva employs more subtle, ambushing methods. Living in a vertical pit with just its chitinised head protruding at ground level, forming a kind of living lid, it waits until a potential victim passes close by and then darts forward, seizing the prey in its powerful mandibles and taking it back into its pit for safe consumption. Were the larva to undertake more open predatory activities it would itself be at considerable risk, since its body is soft and unarmoured to allow for easier development.

Tiger-beetles belong to a large group, the Carabidae, which includes many species that actively hunt, mainly at night. Some of these so-called ground-beetles are especially active after rain, which brings out the worms,

Many ants are confirmed predators, using numbers to attack and overcome their prey with a combination of stings and bites. These *Aphaenogaster tennesseensis* are attacking a caterpillar in Tennessee deciduous forest.

snails and slugs on which they prey. The European *Carabus violaceus* is among several species popularly called 'rain-beetles' because of their association with wet conditions, which their daytime appearance has long been supposed to foretell. Other ground-beetles seek their prey underground, among them the resplendent *Carabus auratus*, which consumes root-feeding cockchafer and other larvae of similar habits. Still more belie their name and climb trees in search of invertebrate prey. The various species of *Calosoma*, handsomely garbed in metallic bronze-green or black, are of particular value to forestry in reducing the numbers of defoliators, such as the caterpillars of green oak tortrix, gypsy and processionary moths, as well as the larvae of sawflies. Ants, too, ascend trees in search of prey, among them the various species of wood ants (*Formica*) and the terrible driver, army or legionary ants, which also scour the ground in their incessant search for food. Curiously, the army ant workers are quite blind, relying principally on scent and sheer numbers to overcome animals, small and large, not quick enough to get out of their way. Depending on its size, prey is overcome by a combination of sting and jaws, larger victims being rent into pieces on the spot.

Other insect predators employ more subtle, individual methods to secure their victims. The praying mantis's predatory approach involves simply waiting on foliage or flowers until the hapless victim – e.g., a grasshopper – comes within range, when it is seized, not in the jaws, but in strongly barbed prehensile forelegs which lock like pincers about the prey while the mantis takes what seem to be inappropriately delicate bites from it, usually discarding legs and wings or pieces of the body found to be less palatable. Mantids tend, in fact, to be rather wasteful feeders and may take only a taste before discarding the bulk of their victim's carcase.

Of all insect predators, mantids are probably among the best equipped for killing prey. Their large widespread eyes bear smaller more visually acute ommatidia in the centre which allow them to pinpoint the position of their prey with extreme accuracy. The eyes, moreover, are positioned on a free-swivelling head which allows the insects to look over their shoulder and follow the victim's movements. In shape and camouflage a mantid is clearly designed for easier prey-approach; it is generally stick- or leaf-like in shape and of varying shades of green or brown, and it heightens this deception by gently swaying its body in evident imitation of breeze-stirred foliage. Some mantids display the most astonishing matching disguises to get within striking range of their prey. The African *Idolum diabolicum*, locally called 'African devil's flower', is so flower-like that flies and butterflies are attracted to it, with frequently fatal results. Other species are able to change their colour pattern as they develop from nymph to adult, in order to match buds and flowers more effectively, or can lighten or darken the colours of their cuticle according to the intensity of the light.

The development of the forelegs as aids to predation is a feature of various other insect groups, among them the curious mantis-flies (Mantispidae), which, like mantids, usually lurk in flowers, and a host of Heteropterid bugs. Assassin-bugs and damsel-bugs hunt on the ground, while others are aquatic. Pond-skaters and water-measurers (which resemble miniature stick-insects), as well as water-crickets, take their prey on the surface of ponds, lakes and sluggish rivers: usually insects, such as mayflies and caddis, that have fallen onto it. Fully aquatic, free-swimming water-scorpions and saucer-bugs, tropical species of which attain a considerable size, have such forward-extending pincer-like forelegs that they appear to be true mandibles. Once seized, the prey is overcome by the injection of a powerfully acting digestive enzyme through the piercing rostrum. Some insects use their forelegs for aerial prey capture. Snipe-flies, Empids and robber-flies are among these flying bandits, some robber-flies being large and powerful enough to capture smaller dragonflies which, in turn, also use their legs to seize prey but in a subtly different fashion. The thoracic segments of dragonflies and damselflies are so positioned that the attached legs bunch together just beneath and forward of the head, enabling them to be used in

Assassin-bugs are among the ground-predators. This unidentified species from Peru is feeding on a *Chromacris* grasshopper whose striking warning colouration has not saved it from death.

Robber-flies are among insect aerial predators. This is a species of *Efferia* which has caught a bee-fly (family Bombyliidae) in the semi-desert of New Mexico, USA.

combination as a bristly insect-trapping basket. The larger dragonflies are highly impressive fliers and proficient hunters and have even been known to swoop down to the water's surface and take small frogs and fish, subsequently chewing them up with their tooth-edged mandibles. Once again, there is considerable difference between the adult dragonfly's method of prey capture and that used by its aquatic nymph. Spending often several years in underwater development, the nymph has hinged to the lower part of its mouth an articulated 'arm', at the extremity of which is a pair of sharp-pointed fangs carried by modified labial palps. When an insect larva, leech, worm or tadpole comes within range, the arm is shot forward by means of increased blood pressure, impaling the victim on the spikes. The device is then retracted, bringing the food to the nymph's chewing mandibles, and neatly folded beneath head and thorax until required for further use. Interestingly, dragonfly nymphs have, like the adults, large compound eyes which give them sufficiently keen vision to assess the distance and position of their prey in an almost stereoscopic fashion. Some nymphs actively roam vegetation in search of food, while others merely lie in wait for potential victims to come near.

Adaptations designed to hold prey securely and to bring it within easier reach of the jaws are obviously of particular value when the quarry is large, highly active and liable to struggle; without such aids a predator might well, more often than not, go hungry! We have already referred to the modification of the forelegs for this purpose and, in some insects, the hind limbs are modified in a similar way. In these so-called hanging-flies (Bittacidae), relatives of the more familiar scorpion-flies but with a preference for warmer climates, the extremity of the hindlegs is in the form of a jack-knife-like device for capturing their victims, which are then brought forward to the mouth. Usually predation is effected while the hunter hangs from vegetation, either by its forelegs or by just one leg, until a moth or other insect flutters by, although hanging-flies can also snatch up their prey in full flight. So specialised have the Bittacidae become in their highly individual method of predation that their hindlegs are virtually useless for ordinary locomotion.

In other insects, quite different parts of the body have become modified and changed from their original role so as to aid in predation. The transparent phantom or glass larvae of *Chaoborus* midges capture minute crustaceans and other prey by means of specially adapted prehensile antennae, which normally function as sensory organs. Earwigs, which are omnivorous rather than the plant-eating pests of popular misconception, are said to impale flies and other insects on their pincer-like cerci or tail appendages. Primitive Japygid bristletails (Diplura) probably use their pincers in a somewhat similar way.

The construction of traps or lures is not often thought of as being a typical insect characteristic. It is commonly believed, for example, that the insects' arthropod relatives, the spiders, have cornered the market so far as webs are concerned, yet some insects have also devised webs for trapping their food, among them the larvae of certain caddis-flies, such as *Hydropsyche*. These free-living, aquatic, non-case-making larvae stretch nets of silken strands between rocks and stones. The nets are artfully positioned so as to catch invertebrates swept downstream by the water current. Unlike spiders, whose silk is produced from anal spinnerets, the trapping strands of the caddis emanate from oral glands; silk from the same source is used to line the tube homes of case-making caddis larvae. Equally ingenious are the luminous larvae of certain Mycetophilid flies which construct pendants of sticky threads on bushes or on the roofs of caves to trap small flying insects initially attracted by the larvae's light. *Arachnocampa luminosa*, which lives in New Zealand's Waitomo caves, is the best known species but a number of others occur in Tasmania, as well as on the mainland of Australia. Locals call these flies 'glow-worms', although they are of course quite unrelated to the sexually dimorphic beetles of that name, although they share a similar method of light production. The only real link between the two lies in the fact that *Arachnocampa*'s light may also have sexual significance (just as it does in *Lampyris*), since both the adult females and their pupae are luminous whereas the males are not.

Apart from the larvae of certain snipe-flies (Rhagionidae), the most famous insect exponents of the simple fall trap are the so-called ant-lions (Myrmeleontidae), a group particularly typical of the tropics, although also occurring in parts of Europe, including some of the Channel Islands. The term 'ant-lion' should, strictly speaking, refer only to the larvae because, although the adults, characterised by their large membraneous wings and curved antennae, are at least partly predacious, it is only their progeny which live up to the epithet and subsist on ants and other insects that blunder into their characteristic conical pits in dry sandy soil. The larva instinctively begins to build itself a trap as soon as it emerges from its egg in the sand, at first creating a conical depression by shuffling backwards in a circular movement and flicking excavated soil over the rim with its head. A small pillar thus builds up in the centre of the pit but this is demolished and cleared by the larva which then puts the finishing touches to its trap before taking up a semi-buried position at its base. Ants and other insects that fall, slip or slide over the edge of the pit are helped to their doom by a fusillade of sand which the ant-lion directs at its intended victim with varying accuracy. Once within reach, the ant is almost certain to succumb to the predator's powerful sickle-like jaws. Despite the possession of large compound eyes, ant-lion larvae would appear to be relatively short-sighted since even inanimate objects may be initially bombarded before the pit-dweller realises its mistake.

Not all ant-lions make pits. Some are hunters on the surface of the ground

Ant-lions – the larvae of large-winged Neuropterans – make pits for trapping their prey. These are from Australia.

while others, such as the long-necked larvae of the so-called butterfly-lions, go halfway as it were by covering themselves in soil with only part of their head and mandibles visible. Equally free-living are the larvae of the closely related green and brown lacewings (Chrysopidae and Hemerobiidae) commonly called aphis-lions because of their preference for feeding on these sap-sucking bugs. Some of these tiny predators have the interesting habit of decking their bristly bodies with the cuticles of past victims or even their own shed skins. As in all Neuroptera larvae, victims are simply sucked dry after being injected with digestive enzymes. The tinsel-winged adults, however, chew up their prey whole. Adult and larval ladybirds (Coccinellidae) display similarly contrasting feeding habits.

External digestion is particularly fascinating in those groups whose larvae feed on snails, such as the glow-worm (*Lampyris noctiluca*) and related species. In this case, the snail's shell forms a convenient receptacle for its own liquefied tissue, which the larva then sucks up like soup. During such a meal, the body of the glow-worm larva inevitably becomes smeared with its victim's substance. This problem is dealt with by an ingenious device – an extrusible, fingered structure with which the larva literally sponges itself down. Various other beetles, of the families Carabidae and Silphidae, also feed on snails, both as adults and larvae, but possess less effective means of giving themselves a subsequent wash and brush up.

It has been mentioned elsewhere that insects consistently fail to conform to any standard pattern of behaviour. We should not be surprised, therefore, to find that even the caterpillars of some species of butterflies and moths have turned predator, although the order as a whole is predominantly plant-eating. The best-known example is the larva of the large blue butterfly (*Maculinea arion*) which feeds, in its later instars, on the larvae of *Myrmica* ants. Another Lycaenid larva, that of the eastern North American *Feniseca tarquinius*, specialises in aphids, while some species of Blastobasiid and Noctuid moths, such as *Eublemma* and *Coccidophaga*, are also predatory, feeding principally on scale-insects. The caterpillar of an Hawaiian pug-moth (*Eupithecia orichloris*) is especially remarkable in that it uses its twig-like appearance and angular stance both to deceive its own enemies and to lure fruit-flies within striking distance; the prey is then seized in the jaws with a sudden twisting lunge of astonishing rapidity. Just how and why such caterpillars have developed their untypical taste is a matter for conjecture. Perhaps it originally came about by accident, much as we might perhaps inadvertently consume a maggot whilst eating fruit, the obvious difference being that the caterpillars liked the unlooked-for flavour and changed their diet accordingly.

Scavengers and Omnivores

Amid all the interest and research surrounding those insects that attack cultivated produce, it is often overlooked just how useful a role others of them

Scarab beetles collect balls of animal dung for their own consumption as well as for their larvae. These *Sisyphus* sp. are rolling a ball of elephant dung in Kenyan grassland.

play in consuming plant and animal waste. By feeding on such material and releasing its chemical constituents, partly via their own excrement, scavenging insects of this sort do much to maintain the richness and organic viability of our soils. Feeders on decaying plants and humus tend to be especially numerous. Raking over the leaf-litter in any deciduous woodland or turning a garden compost heap is almost certain to reveal some of the most typical waste-feeders in the shape of tiny springtails which respond to disturbance of their hitherto peaceful pabulum by leaping wildly in all directions. These Collembola are probably the most numerous, in populations, of all soil-dwelling insects, although other primitive groups, such as Proturans and bristletails, as well as tiny beetles and a host of larvae, will be there, too, often in considerable numbers – all of them satisfied with the simplest of fare.

As it is only partly digested, animal dung is another frequent target for many insects, as food either for themselves or for their larvae. A freshly deposited cowpat, for example, is almost certain to attract a myriad flies, among them the yellow-haired dung-fly, *Scatophaga stercoraria*, which deposits its eggs therein and may also take the opportunity to prey on the other flies. Cow, horse, sheep and other animal droppings are also likely to provide food for tiny rove-beetles, as well as much larger ones, such as the European *Emus hirtus*, a handsome species clothed in a yellowish pubescence. Sturdy, shiny black dor-beetles (*Geotrupes*) lay their eggs in short passages beneath heaps of ordure, stocking each with a supply of dung, as does the closely related but far more elusive minotaur (*Typhaeus typhoeus*), the male of which is distinctively armed with forward-pointing thoracic horns. Their kinsmen, the scarab-beetles, include a number of species of more extrovert behaviour – laboriously rolling large balls of animal dung to specially prepared holes, some for their own consumption, others for their larvae.

The infrequency with which one sees dead small mammals and birds lying about in the countryside is a tribute to other insect scavengers that, to a greater or lesser degree, specialise in their consumption. In addition to infesting fresh meat that has been overlong exposed, bluebottles (*Calliphora*) and flesh-flies (*Sarcophaga*) are usually quickly on the scene of a wild animal's death, the former depositing eggs and the latter typically legless larvae on its flesh. *Sarcophaga* larvae, a favourite angler's bait, attain a considerable size and may form a seething wriggling mass giving off a sound reminiscent of gently frying fat! Such heavy infestations may inhibit invasion by other corpse-consumers, but normally a dead animal is the target of a variety of insect scavengers, more especially carrion beetles (Silphidae). Of these, the large sexton- or burying-beetles, equipped as they are with sensitive, multi-branched antennae, have an especially keen appreciation of death and home in on a dead animal as soon as it begins to putrefy and broadcast its sweetness on the air. Such beetles are unpleasant to handle since they have the smell of corruption about them even when separated from their feast of death! Commonly all-black or with conspicuous orange-red bands on the elytra,

Fleshflies, bluebottles and greenbottles lay their eggs in rotting flesh, which the larvae consume. These *Lucilia* fly maggots are feeding on the flesh of a dead rabbit.

Scorpion-flies (Panorpidae) are principally scavengers on dead insects and other animals as well as waste materials. This female *Panorpa communis* is feeding on a moth captured and enshrouded in a spider's web. England/Europe.

sexton-beetles may feed on some of the flesh themselves but their primary interest in it is as food for their larvae. Gradually digging away the soil beneath it, and chewing and manipulating the flesh into a more manageable shape, they contrive to literally bury the corpse so as to make it less of an obvious target for other rival scavengers; after this they lay their eggs in passages leading directly from and to the carrion, so that all the larvae have to do is follow their noses. Such beetles display a primitive form of social behaviour in that they initially feed the young larvae on liquid chyme, derived from semi-digestion of the decomposing flesh. One of the interesting features of waste-feeding beetles lies in their regular infestation with tiny brownish mites which cluster about their undersides in varying numbers. These do not harm the beetles but are carried by them from one food source to another; in the interim they prey on minute waste-feeders, such as fly larvae and worms, which live in the dung and carrion.

Of all insects, probably the most successful – and often difficult to eradicate – are those which we might describe as displaying an almost total lack of discrimination over their diet. These scavenging omnivores include a variety of species which are commonly commensals of man, such as cockroaches, house-crickets and house-moths. Cockroaches, among them the cosmopolitan *Blatta orientalis*, display such wide-ranging appetites that

Butterflies commonly drink up moisture from wet ground, including places where animals have urinated, probably to obtain valuable salts. This Heliconiid (*Philaethria dido dido*) from Peru is feeding on damp ground.

almost nothing of even partly organic origin is safe from their attentions, from old boots and ink to whitewash and photographic film. Equally omnivorous, house-crickets (*Acheta domesticus*) are known to nibble at woollen clothing in addition to consuming household scraps, while larvae of the brown house-moth (*Hoffmannophila pseudopretella*) consume flour, carpets and furnishings, bottle corks and may even burrow into plastics and polythene – presumably en route to something rather more nourishing! The much despised earwig (*Forficula auricularia*) is another insect with varied gastronomic tastes: a partial predator, it will also eat dead insects, nibble at the flesh of dead mammals and birds, chew plant foliage and pollen and invade the household for scraps, which may vary from breadcrumbs to soap.

The need for moisture and the nutritive elements, including chemical salts, that it contains sometimes leads insects into sampling liquids that are either waste or the by-products of decomposition. Fallen fruits, such as plums, are often a great favourite with wasps and Vanessid butterflies, which gorge on their fermenting juices until they become literally drunk. Tropical swallowtails and 'whites' commonly crowd to drink from the borders of rivers and streams where larger animals urinate. The European purple emperor (*Apatura iris*) belies its regal appearance by displaying similar tendencies – frequently sipping from puddles or semi-liquid manure in woodland glades. In excessively dry summers, insects may behave rather out of character by alighting on people's bodies to suck sweat and perhaps incidentally nip the flesh, as did crowds of moisture-seeking ladybirds during the 1976 drought in Britain.

Some of the strangest inveterate seekers after moisture are the various moths and butterflies that imbibe the tears (lachrymal fluid) from the eyes of various animals. Heliconiid butterflies, for example, suck the 'crocodile tears' of South American caymans as they float in the water and are extremely persistent in such endeavours. Cattle and deer are similarly attended by Noctuid moths and one species, the South-East Asian *Calpe eustrigata*, has taken such habits a stage further by piercing the skin and sucking the blood of various mammalian hosts, a characteristic which leads us conveniently to our last category of insect feeders, the parasites, which will be discussed in the next chapter.

Chapter 7
Parasites and Parasitoids

Parasitic insects fall into two more or less distinct categories, according to the degree with which they affect their unwilling hosts. *True parasites* only rarely kill their victims, although they may cause them considerable discomfort and even transmit disease which may eventually result in their death. *Parasitoids*, by contrast, are essentially predators, living within the tissues of their hosts – principally other insects – in such a subtle way that the latter's demise is postponed until the interlopers have completed their larval development.

Blood-Suckers

Some of the most familiar parasitic insects are, naturally enough, those that bite man and suck his blood. They include mosquitoes, horse-flies, biting-midges, black-flies (Simulidae), fleas, lice and bed-bugs, all of which have their mouthparts adapted for piercing and sucking, although subtle differences in individual structure are displayed. In mosquitoes the proboscis is a marvellously intricate structure (see Fig. 6.2) consisting of six different stylets, each adapted for a particular purpose – for making the primary incision, inserting anti-coagulant and digestive enzymes contained in the insect's saliva and, finally, withdrawing the blood itself. All the stylets are secreted within a protective sheath formed by the labium or lower lip, which, during blood extraction, is slid up out of the way into a loop form. In each group of insect phlebotomists, the injection of anti-coagulant to prevent blood-clotting (the natural reaction when the skin is pierced) is crucial since, without it, the sucker's mouthparts would become clogged and unworkable. It is presumably salivary injections of this sort that cause much of the irritation ensuing from insect blood-letting, which varies in degree from one individual to another. Those people with mild allergies are likely to suffer particular discomfort and so are profuse perspirers, since any increase in body temperature and humidity, which is accompanied by heightened emanations of carbon dioxide, constitutes an open invitation to host-sensitive attackers.

Most Dipterid blood-suckers are not true parasites since they merely visit mammals, birds, reptiles and amphibians for a meal of blood and do not live a settled existence on their bodies in the way that fleas, lice and bed-bugs do. With these aerial attackers, the old adage about the female being more

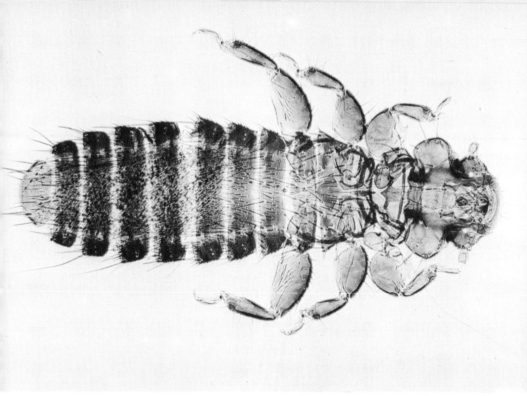

Mallophaga are principally ectoparasites of birds, feeding on skin fragments, dermal secretions and, occasionally, blood. This one, *Actornithophilus ochraceus*, was taken from a redshank.

A notorious blood-sucking commensal of man – the bed-bug (*Cimex lectularius*).

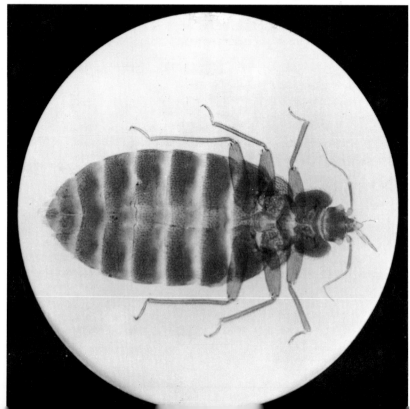

deadly than the male is entirely appropriate since only the females extract blood, both for food and the proper maturation of their eggs; males on the other hand either do not feed at all or content themselves with occasional sips of nectar. By contrast, both sexes of fleas, lice and bed-bugs are blood-suckers and, in the case of the lice and bugs, the nymphs are also, as one would expect of hemimetabolous insects. Flea larvae subsist on organic debris, including the blood-rich droppings of the adults, but develop rapidly and, as pupae, display a marvellous facility for instant emergence as adults as soon as a suitable host appears. This is precisely why a house can still contain a lively flea population, even when the human or other hosts have been absent from it for months. Nor are those fleas usually considered as specific to domestic cats and dogs averse to transferring their attentions to human beings from time to time, as the writer knows to his cost! On the whole, though, mammals and birds tend to possess their own particular species of flea. Hedgehog fleas (*Archaeopsylla erinacei*) frequently infest their prickly hosts in considerable numbers but only rarely transfer their attentions to other mammals or man. The temptation to seek pastures new would be more understandable where the parasite is particularly large in comparison with its host. *Hystrichopsylla talpae*, for example, is a giant among fleas, attaining a length of some 6 mm ($\frac{1}{4}$ in), yet it seems perfectly content with small mammals, ranging from moles to voles and shrews. Just how much discomfort a tiny shrew experiences from having parasites a tenth of its own body length sucking its blood we can only speculate, but perhaps it accepts the situation as one of life's unavoidable hazards. Certain South-East Asian bats must have to develop a similar philosophy, since their situation is often even more unpleasant. Some of them play unwilling host to a species of aberrant earwig (*Arixenia esau*), which is 25 mm (1 in) long, although the bats themselves are only the size of small mice!

The bed-bugs mentioned earlier are by no means the only members of the Heteroptera to subsist on the blood of vertebrate animals. Some specialise in bird hosts, among them being the martin bug (*Oeciacus hirundinis*), which parasitises house martins, swallows and swifts, as well as other cavity-nesting birds, such as sparrows and woodpeckers. Other species may be pests of domestic poultry. Some assassin-bugs (Reduviidae) also suck blood, including man's, in addition to piercing and feeding on the tissues of various invertebrates. The large *Reduvius personatus* invades houses in Europe and North America and has been afforded the tongue-in-cheek name of 'kissing-bug' because of its habit of attacking human residents about the face, usually while they are asleep. It has a saving grace, though, in that it numbers bed-bugs among its insect victims! Another assassin-bug, *Triatoma megista*, is among several species which transmit Chagas's disease, which is especially prevalent in Central and South America. Just as in malaria- and yellow fever-carrying mosquitoes, the blood-sucker is not the direct cause of the disease but merely acts as its carrier – the real culprit, in this case, being the trypanosome (Protozoa) contained in the insect's blood.

Endoparasites

All of the blood-suckers or tissue-suckers so far mentioned are *ectoparasites*, i.e., they merely visit or attach themselves to their host's body surface for the purposes of feeding. Still more unpleasant for the animals thus afflicted are those *endoparasites* that burrow into the flesh to feed or lay their eggs. The jiggers or chigoe fleas (*Tunga penetrans*) of parts of the southern USA, South America and Africa, are particularly noxious in their effects on human hosts, although their behaviour is such as to perhaps label them as semi-endoparasites. Normally, the young females, as well as males, content themselves with an external blood-sucking existence. Gravid females, on the other hand, seem to require richer fare and burrow into the flesh, commonly beneath the toenails, where they gorge on blood until their eggs mature, the whole forming a boil-like sore. Normally the female leaves the wound, or is forcibly expelled, before laying her eggs, since the larvae are principally debris-eaters, like those of other Siphonaptera.

Other insects are fully endoparasitic in that they complete their whole life cycle either in the host's flesh or in the digestive system, although the adults are free-living. Warble-flies (*Hypoderma*) oviposit on the skin or hairs of domestic cattle, the larvae burrowing into the skin to form 'warbles' or swellings on the sufferer's back. Related species, such as the sheep-nostril fly, take a short cut to parasitisation by depositing fully formed larvae in the nostrils of sheep. Equal ingenuity is displayed by *Dermatobia hominis*, which parasitises man in addition to various domestic animals. Instead of directly ovipositing on a host, it seizes a female mosquito and lays its eggs on her, so that the ectoparasitic blood-sucker acts as a carrier – the warble's eggs being induced to hatch by the host's body heat when the mosquito arrives to feed.

Some endoparasitic insects depend on being taken into the host's digestive system in order to complete their larval development. Flies of the family Gasterophilidae, for example, lay their eggs on various mammals, notably horses, in such a position that the host ingests them when it licks its body, perhaps to relieve irritation. On hatching, the larva attaches itself to the horse's stomach lining and feeds on its contents, much in the way that tapeworms do. Having attained full size, the larva allows itself to be expelled with the horse's excreta, completing its pupation in the ground. Some such parasites are of considerable size, with hosts to match, such as species of *Gyrostigma* and *Cobboldia*, which live in the stomach and intestines of rhinoceros and elephant respectively, occasionally in great numbers. Calf elephants seem particularly prone to such parasitisation and not infrequently have their stomachs literally full of *Cobboldia* larvae.

Parasitoids

As mentioned earlier, parasitoid insects are those that not merely take some of their host's substance but kill it in the process, principally by completing

This pale tussock moth (*Dasychira pudibunda*) pupa has been completely hollowed out by the endoparasitic larva of an ichneumon wasp.

their life cycle within its body. Such an extreme outcome is scarcely surprising since the parasitoid's usual victims are other arthropods, especially other insects, and the infiltrator's internal inroads may well eventually reduce the host to little more than a hollow shell. At the same time, these essential predators display a subtlety of feeding that tends to link them with true parasites. In most cases, they instinctively avoid consuming the host's own life support system, so as to keep it alive and therefore fresh for as long as possible – until, that is, the parasitoid has pupated.

By far the most numerous parasitoid insects are the so-called Chalcid, Braconid and ichneumon 'flies' – all members of the order Hymenoptera and therefore better called wasps, although they display very different habits from the social Vespidae. They vary greatly in their choice of victims, laying their eggs on or in the eggs, larvae and pupae of butterflies and moths, beetles, aphids, grasshoppers and many others, in addition to spiders. Chalcids tend to specialise in one particular stage in their hosts' life history and some are so small as to be able to oviposit in the eggs of insects as small or smaller than themselves. *Alaptus magnanimus*, for example, is so minute – a mere 0.2 mm ($\frac{8}{1000}$ in) – that it is able to choose the eggs of Psocid lice, themselves scarcely visible to the unaided eye, as hosts for its larvae. Others have become so specialised in their choice of victims that they are able to swim under water and seek out the eggs of various water-bugs for parasitisation. One of the most familiar Braconids, at least in its effects, is *Apanteles glomeratus*, which parasitises the caterpillars of the large white butterfly (*Pieris brassicae*) – a considerable pest of cabbages in many parts of the world. *Apanteles* lays its eggs on the caterpillar's cuticle, the larvae burrowing inside and eventually pupating on its surface within a mass of yellow cocoons. Anyone growing brassicas in quantity will surely be familiar with such evidence of pest parasitisation and will welcome it accordingly. However, since the caterpillars have usually finished feeding and are intent on seeking a place to pupate when they are finally killed, the Braconids' primary effect, from the viewpoint of biological control, is to reduce the numbers of a new generation of egg-laying adults. It is, as we saw earlier, very much in the parasites' interest – if not man's! – to ensure that their hosts are alive and feeding for as long as possible. Sometimes endoparasitisation does not even prevent a larva from pupating but it certainly brings a firm halt to the production of the adult.

Some of the most striking parasitoid insects are members of the family Ichneumonidae, which includes species both small and large and popularly regarded with suspicion because of the frequently exceedingly long, needle-like ovipositor which the female carries. Needless to say, such an appendage has a very specific purpose and is rarely, if ever, used for purposes other than egg-laying, unless deliberately man-handled. In the large European *Rhyssa persuasoria*, the female employs her ovipositor to almost incredible effect in parasitising the wood-feeding larvae of horntails or wood-wasps which, despite their name, are close relatives of the sawflies. *Rhyssa* may attain a total length of about 80 mm (3 in), but considerably more than half of this is ovipositor which she is able to thrust, with uncanny precision, into the trunk of a pine tree and onto the surface (or into the feeding gallery) of the wood-wasp larva. The North American *Thalessa* (*Megarhyssa*) is even more astonishingly endowed, having an ovipositor up to 150 mm (6 in) long! Precisely how these insects manage to insert their exceedingly delicate egg-laying tools deep into solid wood is by no means fully understood. Equally remarkable is the accuracy with which the ichneumons locate their prey in the first place. Presumably, they pick up the vibrations transmitted by the larva's movements through their feet and body and are also guided to it by scent, but the whole process of parasitisation in such groups displays a combination of extreme sensitivity and precision that is way beyond human experience and comprehension.

In those parasitoids that choose other predators as hosts for their larvae, it is often only their small size and agility which saves them from paying for their boldness with their lives. Ant-like females of the Tiphiid genus *Methoca* easily evade the massive jaws of burrow-living tiger-beetle larvae and lay a single egg on their unprotected bodies after paralysing them with their stings; they may even spend the night in the larva's burrow and then seal it up after their work is accomplished. *Methoca*'s provision for her larva's future must frequently involve her in a good deal of footwork, since she is wingless, although other much larger 'solitary' wasps are fully winged and spend their time hovering and running over the ground in search of suitable prey. Spider-hunting wasps (Pompilidae) specialise in spiders, some of them of considerable size, which they sting into submission and drag off to a specially prepared larval chamber – in most cases their victims being far too heavy to be carried in flight. Such a procedure can in itself bring danger for the Pompilid as it may well be challenged by marauding ants or adult tiger-beetles while transporting its victim. Still greater risk is run by giant spider-hunting wasps of the South American genus *Pepsis*. They are large insects, with an average body length of some 80 mm (3 in), and a powerful sting capable of killing small rodents. They need to be well armed, as well as agile, for they seek out huge mygalomorph spiders as big as a hand, entering their burrows to sting them. The spiders do not submit without a fight and frequently a titanic struggle may ensue, lasting some hours, before the wasp is able to overcome its formidable foe; almost invariably the wasp is the victor, but there must be times when the tables are turned and the aggressor falls victim to its intended prey. In most cases, the wasp's first move is to sting the spider in the region of the head, so as to put its vast jaws out of action, and then to administer further paralysis-inducing injections at greater leisure.

Apart from the Hymenoptera, the only other insects to undergo their metamorphosis as parasitoids are certain true flies (Diptera), of which the Tachinidae are the most important. Characterised by their strongly bristled thorax and abdomen, these otherwise rather undistinguished-looking flies parasitise almost all other insect orders, as well as other arthropods, such as centipedes and scorpions, and even worms and snails. Members of the

Some ichneumon flies, or wasps, are able to insert their long ovipositors deep into the trunks of trees in order to lay their eggs in or on the larva of a wood wasp. This *Rhysella curvipes* is ovipositing in an alder to parasitise the larva of the alder wood wasp (*Xiphyoria camelus*). It is a close relative of *Rhyssa persuasoria* which parasitises *Urocerus* and *Sirex* wood wasps. England/Britain.

Oil-beetles (Meloidae) parasitise the eggs and larvae of various other insects, including aculeate Hymenoptera (bees and wasps) and grasshoppers. Their larvae feed within the eggs or larvae. This is an adult *Lytta magister* from Arizona, USA. The larva is hypermetamorphic.

Conopidae or thick-headed flies, some of which are wasp-like in shape and colouring, are slightly less wide-ranging in their choice of hosts, tending to specialise in various bees, wasps and grasshoppers. Some Conopids, such as the large Neotropical *Stylogaster*, take advantage of the confusion caused by army ants on the march to lay their eggs on fleeing insects, such as crickets and cockroaches. Others even go so far as to parasitise the ants themselves.

Some insect endoparasitisation of other insects is difficult to classify, since it does not invariably result in the death of the host, although it may produce side effects, such as sterilisation. Larvae of the little-known Stylopids, tiny insects once classified with the beetles, afford an example of these semi-parasitoids. These larvae lurk in a flower-head until a suitable host, such as a solitary bee, wasp or fly, arrives; they then attach themselves to a host and burrow into its abdomen, where they complete their development. If the parasite proves to be a male, it leaves its host via a hole in the forepart of the abdomen and flies off on its single pair of wings to seek a female. She needs to be sought in the body of another host, for she never leaves her larval home and, indeed, is incapable of so doing, being both legless and wingless and also blind. Once mated, the female produces a large batch of eggs within the bee's body, after which she dies. The larvae then seek their freedom and fresh hosts when the unwitting carrier visits a flower to feed. The curious thing is that the host not merely survives the Stylopid's inroads on its body but can even repair the gap in its abdominal cuticle left by the parasite's exit. Oil-beetles (Meloidae), which include the famous blister beetle or 'Spanish fly' (*Lytta vesicatoria*), have a somewhat similar life history except that the triungulin larvae merely use the adult insects as carriers, after which they feed on their hosts' eggs or larvae. Both they and Stylopids display an additionally interesting feature in that their larvae occur in two quite distinct forms. The early so-called triungulin larva is highly active, since it needs to cling to a flower-visiting insect; once within the latter's tissues, however, it loses its legs and becomes totally sedentary. Such *hypermetamorphosis* occurs in several other insect groups, though in different circumstances.

Hyperparasitism

Since we have already established that 'dog-eat-dog' is very much a part of the pattern of insect behaviour, it is not surprising to find that many parasitic insects are also *hyperparasitic*, i.e. they attack and subsist on other parasites. One of the best-known examples is that of the tiny ichneumon, *Hemiteles*, which lays its eggs in caterpillars already afflicted by larvae of the larger *Apanteles*. These produce adults from the yellow cocoons of *Apanteles* attached to the outside of the caterpillar's husk. More involved still is the life history of *Perilampus hyalinus*, which begins life as an egg laid on the caterpillar of species of North American tiger-moth (*Hyphantria*). On hatching, it bores its way inside and, if the caterpillar has already been parasitised by a Tachinid or ichneumon, feeds on one or more of its larvae as an endoparasite. Nor is that the end of the story, for *Perilampus* is also hypermetamorphic – making its way out of the caterpillar's body to complete its larval development on its surface as a legless ectoparasite, quite different in structure from its original form.

Hyperparasitism also occurs in a variety of other groups, such as bee-flies (Bombylidae), adults of which are like long-tongued bees, as well as in certain gall growths, which sometimes contain a whole succession of parasites feeding on each other. A kind of hyperparasitism might also be said to occur in the 'semi-parasitic' blood-sucking flies with which we began this chapter. Ceratopogonid midges, in addition to sucking the tissues of a variety of other insects, frequently waylay and rob engorged mosquitoes of their blood-cargo, although they are perfectly capable of carrying out the primary business for themselves.

Social Parasites

Defended as they are by a host of stinging, biting or spraying guards, perfectly ready to sacrifice themselves for the sake of the community as a whole, the nests of social insects (Chapter 10) would seem unprofitable and dangerous places for other insects to invade. Yet they, too, do not escape the attention of parasites. A whole host of insects take their lives in their hands by invading the nests of ants, bees, wasps and termites for food or purposes of parasitisation and many go further and take up permanent residence there, some of them having become such specialised commensals that they can exist nowhere else.

Not all such interlopers are harmful to the nest community. Some exist as scavengers on scraps of food or waste or discarded larval skins and are consequently largely tolerated; others, more sinister in their activities, manage to survive because of their minute size, which may enable them to live in small tunnels leading from the legal occupants' main passages, or by exuding substances which either repel attack or are accepted as sweet bribes. A number of intruders imitate their hosts' shape and behaviour as a means of going their way unmolested.

A large proportion of these tiny intruders are Staphylinid beetles, but they include representatives of a great many other insect orders, e.g. bristletails, springtails, book-lice, crickets, bugs, wingless flies, Tineid moth larvae and many more. The bristletail, *Atelura*, is a particularly bold interloper in that it endeavours to take sips of liquid food being mutually exchanged between two ant workers; *Lomechusa*, a species of rove-beetle, is scarcely less intrepid in that it stimulates an ant worker to regurgitate food by tapping its head with its forefeet in evident imitation of another ant. *Claviger*, another rove-beetle, even goes so far as to eat the queen ant's eggs as they are being laid, clinging to her abdomen to accomplish its design. Paussid beetles, notable for their large leaf-like antennae, repay their ant hosts' hospitality by attacking and disembowelling them; strangely the ants do not seem to resist but even adopt a helpful submissive attitude while being devoured. Like many such nest intruders, the beetles exude a sweet-tasting substance from abdominal glands which the ants eagerly lick, but this would seem scarcely sufficient reason for tolerating such liberties. Indeed, it is clear that the social hosts are in some way inhibited from taking revenge on such dangerous parasites –

Velvet-ants are not true ants but 'cuckoo' wasps (family Mutillidae), whose wingless females wander over the ground in search of bumble bees and other aculeates, whose larvae they parasitise by laying their eggs in them or in their cells. This *Hoplomutilla opima* was photographed in a forest in Trinidad.

many of which they carefully rear along with their own brood, not infrequently to its detriment!

The social community's tolerance of such intrusions is remarkable enough, but some species of painfully-stinging *Myrmica* ants seem even more intent on being their own worst enemies. They deliberately incur parasitisation of their brood by taking down semi-carnivorous caterpillars of various 'blue' butterflies into their nests. In the case of the large blue (*Maculinea arion*), the young caterpillars begin by feeding on the flowers of wild thyme but, after several moults, become restless, as if seeking alternative sustenance. The worker ants are initially stimulated into transporting the caterpillars underground by licking a glandular secretion from the upper part of their guests' thorax. Once in the nest, the caterpillars wax fat on their changed diet of ant larvae, pupate and, on emergence as adults, crawl out to the open air. That the large blue caterpillars already possess a carnivorous propensity before they ever meet up with the ants is indicated by the fact that they tend to be cannibalistic on members of their own kind when on their food plants.

Since their nests tend to be rather more permanent affairs than those of bees and wasps, ant and termite communities display a wider variety of insect 'guests' than those of other social groups. Several thousand species of more or less permanent residents of this kind have been identified – classified by such authorities as the myrmecologist, W.M. Wheeler, according to their varying relationship with their hosts. Other kinds of intruders tend to employ a somewhat different approach and visit the social insects' domain simply to lay their eggs on the hosts' larvae and then, if they can, quickly make their way out again. Female Mutillid wasps, commonly called 'velvet ants', invade the nests of bumble-bees, as well as various solitary wasps, to oviposit on their larvae; some species of hover-fly (*Volucella*) parasitise *Bombus* in a similar way, the larvae also living in their nests as scavengers.

Still more drastic, even cataclysmic, in effect are the activities of various social bees, wasps and ants which actually take over the nests of other species and commandeer their larvae into working for them. Queen *Psithyrus* bees, larger and more strongly built than their hosts, may kill the resident bumble queen and some of her workers before being accepted; they subsequently lay eggs which are then reared as if they were those of the original queen. Principally, *Psithyrus* acts in this way because she lacks pollen baskets on her hind legs and is thus unable to gather the pollen so essential for founding a colony on her own. *Vespula austriaca* and other so-called cuckoo-wasps take over the nests of some social wasps in a somewhat similar way but for a rather different reason, i.e. they do not possess a true worker caste. Some species of ants also make a habit of commandeering other species' communities.

Bees and wasps may also suffer far more insidious attacks, directed at the very homes they labour so long to construct. Larvae of the notorious cosmopolitan wax moth (*Galleria mellonella*) not merely eat their hosts' larvae, as well as cast skins and miscellaneous waste, but burrow into their combs to consume the wax. They may also attack the papery combs of social wasps. The lesser wax moth (*Achroia grisella*) is another species with similar habits. The damage these moths do to honey-bee combs is often considerable, especially in warmer climates, although in some situations they may perhaps be considered beneficial in destroying old abandoned combs and dead broods which might otherwise spread disease.

Chapter 8
Life Histories

The growth and development of an insect from egg to adult takes two main forms. In the *hemimetabolous* Apterygote and Exopterygote insects (see orders on pp. 184–198), eggs produce young larvae which are commonly referred to as nymphs (naiads in dragonflies) since, unlike the larvae of the Endopterygota, they are basically similar to the adult except for their size, inability to breed and, in those with adults able to fly, lack of wings, which are present only as buds. The adult insect emerges from the fully grown nymph, which remains fully active until this change takes place. Since insects of this type lack a true larval stage, they are said to display *direct* or *incomplete metamorphosis* to distinguish them from the *holometabolous* Endopterygote insects whose life history is slightly more involved. Insects of these orders (pp. 198–210) lay eggs which produce larvae quite different in form from the adult, examples being the multi-legged caterpillar of a butterfly or moth and the legless larva of a fly. When full-size, such larvae undergo a further change

The male vapourer moth (*Orygia antiqua*) seeks out the wingless female with the aid of his strongly developed antennae.

The female vapourer moth is wingless and waits on her pupal cocoon until visited by a male. After mating, she lays a large batch of eggs over her cocoon. The larvae, once hatched, disperse to their food plants.

Full-grown (last instar) larvae of the vapourer moth. The larger caterpillar will produce a female moth – a case of pre-adult sexual dimorphism.

of form to become a pupa or chrysalis which, unlike the fully grown nymph of Exopterygote insects, is either totally inert or capable of only limited movement, and certainly does not feed. Final transformation to adult involves yet another complete revision of both internal and external structure whereas in insects displaying *indirect or complete metamorphosis* such changes are less radical.

Egg Stage

The eggs of insects vary considerably in shape, size and number and also in the degree of protection afforded to them. Some butterflies, moths and

European ruddy darter dragonfly (*Sympetrum sanguineum*). The female (lower) drops her eggs into the water while flying in tandem, attached to the brilliantly coloured male.

An Australian shieldbug (*Tectocoris diophthalmus*) of the family Scutelleridae guarding her egg-batch.

Phasmids merely drop them on the ground at random, while many aquatic groups, such as mayflies and dragonflies, release them into the water where they may well be consumed by predators before they hatch. A variety of insects deposit their eggs quite openly on vegetation, either in ones or twos or in large close-packed batches, although the ova are frequently cryptically coloured to lessen the chances of detection. Other eggs are given a somewhat more secure start to life by being inserted into the stems of plants (as in bush-crickets) or, as in the many parasitic insects, into the tissues of other animals. Eggs of body lice, commonly called 'nits', are attached to the body hairs of the host by a cement-like substance. Those of lacewings and mantis-flies (Neuroptera) are positioned at the end of long threads, at least partly to deter the first hatchers from eating the others. In some groups, such as cockroaches, mantids and grasshoppers, the ova are enclosed in a spongy substance to form a cocoon or *ootheca*. Direct care of the eggs is not a common insect trait but it does occur in various Pentatomid bugs, earwigs, some crickets, Japygid bristletails and others.

Adult female insects emerge from the fully grown nymph or pupa with a full complement of eggs, retained in the ovaries; these, in general, must be fertilised by a male before oviposition. However, it is not uncommon for female moths, for example, to deposit infertile eggs automatically in certain circumstances, notably when attracted to artificial light, while some insects are able to lay eggs which hatch without fertilisation (see p. 113). In the more primitive insects, notably the Apterygota, fertilisation of the eggs is external; some springtails, for example, deposit packets of sperm in strategic positions which the female then takes up into her genital opening. In most cases, however, fertilisation is direct, the male inserting his intromittent *aedegus* into the fe male and injecting sperm either freely or, more usually, in the form of a capsule. The female has a special sperm-retaining structure (*spermatheca*) from which she is able to release sperm to fertilise the eggs as they pass along the oviduct and out through the egg-laying device (ovipositor). The latter is sometimes extremely conspicuous, as in bush-crickets and ichneumon wasps, while in other groups, such as grasshoppers, it is only extruded when the eggs are laid in the soil. The eggs have a tough shell, called a *chorion*, with a minute aperture or *micropyle* on some part of their surface, often within an indentation, through which the male's sperm enters.

Larval Emergence and Development

While in the egg, the embryo insect larva grows by feeding on liquid yolk. It eventually frees itself to begin its external existence by various means. In some groups, such as stick-insects, there is a line of easy fracture, enabling the top of the egg to be pushed up like a lid; in others, there may be a special spine or *egg-burster* on the larva's head, thorax or abdomen; others simply chew their way out. Commonly, too, the emergent larva brings tension to bear on the egg shell by muscular movement and by swallowing fluid within the egg, which has the effect of drawing in air through the micropyle.

These larvae of the pot-bellied emerald beetle (*Gastrophysa viridula*, family Chryso-melidae) are eating their egg-shells after hatching. England/Europe.

One of the first actions of many emergent larvae is to eat at least a part of their egg shell, which is of a proteinous nature; indeed, such an initial meal seems quite essential to the well-being of many larvae, especially the caterpillars of butterflies and moths. In any case, the young insect's sole purpose now is to feed and grow. Methods of feeding are discussed in Chapter 6 and the main point to be mentioned here is that growth is not continuous, as in mammals and birds, but must be accompanied by periodic shedding of the whole cuticle, the process known as ecdysis. The cuticle of the larva (or nymph) is elastic but capable of only limited expansion, so that at intervals of 'repletion', it ceases to feed and takes up an immobile position to allow ecdysis to take place. To understand this process, it must first be appreciated that the larva's skin consists of several layers: an outer cuticle (which is to be shed), overlying an inner endocuticle, which covers an epidermal layer. When the cuticle is ready to be shed, secretion of a special moulting fluid by glands in the epidermal layer is triggered off by means of hormones. This dissolves the endocuticle, thus producing a gap between cuticle and epidermis. All the larva now has to do is to ease itself out of the old skin; this is frequently a somewhat lengthy and hazardous business, since the insect is completely defenceless against the attacks of predators while thus engaged. It is aided by the secretion of lubricating fluid, which gives the larva's new cuticle a glossy appearance, as well as by swallowing air and by the pumping action of the blood, which brings tension to bear on the outer skin. Rupture of the outer skin is commonly made between the lobes of the head or along the median line of the thorax, although, in some cases, partial freedom is gained by pushing the head capsule off whole. Like the egg shells, the shed cuticle may be eaten by the larva.

For some time after ecdysis, the insect larva remains inactive, so that blood can be pumped into the outer skin layer and various toughening processes can take place in the cuticle, which starts by being soft and commonly colourless. It then resumes feeding until a further ecdysis becomes necessary. The number of cuticle changes varies considerably from insect to insect, as does the length of larval life. In some Chalcid wasps, the whole cycle from egg to adult may be completed in about a week, whereas in others, such as stoneflies, there can be as many as thirty or more moults over a larval period of some 3 years. Undoubtedly the record length of larval life is displayed by the American periodical cicada (*Magicicada septemdecim*), which spends either 13 or 17 years as a subterranean, root-feeding nymph; yet, curiously, the nymph passes through only seven *instars* or *stadia* in this long period of time.

Larval types vary considerably. Many, including the caterpillars of butterflies and moths and the superficially similar larvae of sawflies, are relatively active, with numbers of false legs or pseudopodia, which are shed during the change to adult. Nymphal grasshoppers are equally as agile as the adults, except in their capacity for flight (wings are present only in the form of gradually developing buds). Such activity is a characteristic feature of most Exopterygote nymphs, notably those of groups such as bugs and cockroaches, whereas a large number of Endopterygote larvae are sluggish and sedentary and some, such as the larvae of true flies and fleas, are legless – limbs being unnecessary since they are surrounded by their food.

Many insect larvae attain a considerable size, in some cases greater than that of the adults. The South American longhorn beetle, *Titanus giganteus*, attains a length of some 150 mm (6 in), and is probably the longest beetle in the world, but its wood-boring larva exceeds it by some 100 mm (4 in). Larvae of the endoparasitic fly, *Gyrostigma*, which lives in the digestive tract of the rhinoceros, are also extremely large. At the other extreme, caterpillars of certain leaf-mining moths are so minute that they can live and feed between the two cuticle layers of a leaf, while some Chalcid fly larvae are even smaller.

Preparation for Adulthood

As we have seen, Exopterygote insects do not pass through a proper pupal stage, but undergo a gradual progression towards the adult form via a series of active, ever larger nymphs, so that the final transformation to adult involves rather less drastic structural reorganisation than it does in Endopterygote groups. In the nymphs of winged insects of this type, the only major external difference between them and adults is the presence of wing buds on the thoracic surface, which become larger with each succeeding moult. In wingless groups undergoing incomplete metamorphosis, the young insect's similarity to the adult is even greater, except for its smaller size and, of course, sexual immaturity. This applies in particular to the four orders of the Apterygota: the springtails, two-pronged and three-pronged bristletails and the Proturans.

By contrast with these, Endopterygote insects (i.e. those undergoing a complete metamorphosis) have evolved a further resting or pupal stage, quite distinct from the actively feeding larva, during which activity ceases entirely and the whole larval structure is broken down and reformed into that of the adult. A glance at the larva of a butterfly or that of a bee will make it obvious that such a pupa stage is necessary since the larvae and adults are structurally very different, in contrast to the nymphs of, say, a grasshopper or bug, which are much closer to the adults.

Broadly speaking, insect pupae are classified into two main groups. The first and more primitive type is called *decticous* (from the Greek word meaning 'tooth') since the pupa possesses movable biting mandibles, commonly used for chewing its way out of a protective cocoon. Insects which have pupae of this type include caddis-flies, scorpion-flies, lacewings, ant-lions and snake-flies. Such pupae also display limbs or limb-casings which are free of the body and not sealed down in an homogeneous whole (see below) and some are consequently capable of varying degrees of activity. Snake-fly pupae, usually to be found in shallow declivities beneath peeling bark, can run about quite freely, especially just prior to adult emergence, and also snap at intruders on their domain with their jaws.

Adecticous ('toothless') pupae do not possess jaws and are quite inert, although some resemble the decticous type in having the head, mouthparts, antennae, wing cases and legs clearly separated or free. Beetles, bees, wasps, ants and flies are among those groups with pupae of this *exarate* type. By contrast, the pupae or chrysalids of butterflies and moths are mostly *obtect*, i.e. with the head, limbs etc. completely enclosed, although the position of these structures is usually clearly defined, with, for example, the wing casings folded round over the ventral surface, below the future antennae. Many adecticous pupae are enclosed in cocoons of varying shape and consistency. That of the puss moth (*Cerura vinula*) is constructed on the boles of willow and sallow and is of extreme toughness, being fashioned from a mixture of labial silk and bark fragments which hardens into an oval whole, rough and bark-like on the outside but glossily smooth inside. Having no biting jaws, pupae of this type need other means to free themselves from their cocoons. The puss moth exudes a special liquid which softens the casing, allowing the moth to push its way out through a relatively small hole; others have special cocoon-rupturing structures on head or thorax which may be lost on emergence.

Apart from a few groups, such as skippers and browns, which make loose silken cocoons, the majority of butterfly pupae are formed without the protection of a cocoon. Many simply hang from a pad of silk attached to the food plant by the tip of the abdomen (e.g. the Vanessids) or are additionally

The pupae of some insects are of the exarate type with 'free' limbs, wing-casings, etc. The pupa of this snakefly (*Raphidia* sp.) is also decticous, with movable biting jaws. The ovipositor sheath, doubled over the back, indicates a future adult female.

Pupa of the eyed hawk-moth (*Smerinthus ocellata*). Butterfly and moth pupae are of the obtect type, with all appendages enclosed within an homogenous covering.

Many moths make protective cocoons in which to pupate. The larva of the puss moth (*Cerula vinula*) makes its cocoon on the trunks of willows and sallows, mixing small pieces of bark with its silk to make a hard camouflaged surface. Here a pupa has been removed from its cocoon for comparison.

Some butterfly pupae have a silken girdle supporting their attachment to leaves and stems, like this *Delias* sp. (family Pieridae) from a Queensland rain forest.

supported by a girdle of silk encircling both stem and pupa, the latter being usually in an upright position (Pierids, Papilionids and Lycaenids).

Adult Emergence

Adult emergence generally takes place along lines of easy fracture along the median line of the thorax and following the curvature of the wings, this area being then pushed off. At first the adult is moist and soft and the wings are merely abbreviated folds of tissue. Gradually, however, the body hardens and the wings expand through blood pressure, muscular movement and the swallowing of air; in most cases the insect hangs body downwards to gain gravitational assistance. One of the new adult's earliest actions is to void excretory fluid, commonly pinkish in colour, accumulated during the pupation period.

The insect that emerges from the pupa or fully grown nymph is not necessarily fully mature. There may be a period of time before the gonads ripen and the insect can mate. Moreover, many newly emerged insects, especially dragonflies, do not assume their full colouration until some days, or even weeks, after emergence. Such immature adults are called *tenerals*. In one insect order, the mayflies, the winged insects that emerge from the aquatic nymphs pass through yet another change of cuticle, and wings and even cerci are shed entire. In all other insects, however, the winged adult undergoes no further moult but is ready to undertake its primary functions in life – mating and egg-laying.

Insect Life Spans

In considering the question of how long insects live, one has to bear in mind that the greater part of their lives is usually spent in the larval form, whereas the adults are commonly extremely short-lived and are really little more than reproductive entities. An extreme example of this seemingly rather

This cryptically camouflaged lappet moth (*Gastropacha quercifolia*) has just emerged from its silken cocoon.

alien phenomenon is presented by the mayflies, which may spend 2–3 years feeding and growing as nymphs at the bottom of a lake or stream and then live but a few hours, or even less, as winged adults. Many beetles may have equally long-lived larvae, among them wood-feeding Lucanids, Cerambycids and Elaterids and waste-consuming Scarabaeids, whereas the adults rarely last more than a few months. The European glow-worm, for example, spends 3 or sometimes 4 years as a larva, hibernating each winter, whereas the adult glowing and mating period is rarely more than a week or two. Probably the lengthiest development period is spent by the periodical cicadas (*Magicicada septemdecim*) of North America. In southern latitudes, the subterranean root-sucking nymphs take 13 years to produce adults, while, further north, the period required is even longer – 17 years.

Perhaps not surprisingly, it is the social insects – the ants, bees and termites – which tend to produce the longest-lived adults. Whereas workers and males are typically ephemeral, the colony-founding queens may survive for a considerable period of time. A queen wood ant (*Formica rufa*) has been kept in captivity for 15 years and may well have been several years older than that

The comma butterfly (*Polygonia c-album*) hibernates during the winter in the adult stage. England.

This green lacewing (*Chrysopa carnea*) commonly overwinters in houses, garden sheds, etc, during which time it loses its green colouration. It is regained on emergence in spring. Europe.

when she died. Queen honey-bees (*Apis mellifera*) probably live for about half that period, while it has been suggested that some termite queens pursue an active mating and egg-laying life for as much as 50 years, barring accidents.

At the other end of the scale, some insects complete their metamorphosis in an incredibly short space of time. Certain species of parasitic Chalcid wasps, for example, take no more than a week to develop from egg to adult, lay their own eggs and die.

Diapause

The earlier reference to hibernation (p. 94) draws attention to the fact that, while insects generally contrive to undergo their life cycles in continuous rotation, unfavourable climatic conditions may artificially as it were prolong their development (and lives) and induce them to go into a state of suspended animation or *diapause*. To some degree, this is an essential element of an insect's metamorphosis. During the pupal stage, for example, the insect is often developing at an exceedingly slow rate, but that condition is still further slowed during very low temperatures, which delay adult emergence. Such hibernation may also occur in the egg, larva (or nymph) or adult stage. Another form of diapause occurs during very dry conditions and is termed *aestivation*. In this state, in extreme cases, insects may remain virtually desiccated for considerable periods of time, sometimes years, as happens to the eggs of desert-living locusts. The larvae of the Dermestid beetle, *Trogoderma granarium*, a near cosmopolitan pest of stored grains, have been recorded as surviving without food and water for as long as 8 years.

The queens are the only members of the social wasps' community to survive the winter. Here a group of queen German wasps (*Vespula germanica*) are hibernating.

Chapter 9
Courtship and Reproduction

It is, as we saw earlier, one of the paradoxes in the life of insects that an often extremely lengthy larval development, perhaps extending over several years, may well produce adults whose active sexual life is extremely brief. Relatively few insects live for more than a year or two as adults (*imagines*) and the majority complete their adult existence in a much shorter period of time – months, weeks, days or even, more especially in some mayflies, hours. Some adult insects do not even feed; indeed many of them, such as mayflies, stoneflies, caddis and some moths, have such aborted mouthparts that they are incapable of taking nourishment. Consequently, it is not surprising to find that insects have devised a wide variety of methods to enable the sexes to find each other with the minimum of fuss and expenditure of time.

Courtship

Rapid recognition of a potential sexual partner is obviously of paramount importance and, in this connection, it is interesting to note that the males and females of many insects are commonly very different in appearance. Such *sexual dimorphism* may be manifested in a wide variety of forms. Often it is simply a matter of colour, female insects being more drab, as well as more retiring in habit than the males, so as to lessen the danger of predation on the more valuable egg-laying sex. The magnificent Morpho butterflies of South America and the smaller 'blues' common throughout much of the Holarctic are famous for their sky blue raiment, but it is the males that attract attention since the females are much less distinctive and, indeed, often more brown than blue.

In other groups, sexual dimorphism involves far greater physical differences. Male Lucanid beetles, such as the European stag-beetle (*Lucanus cervus*), have vast mandibles, useless for feeding, although they may be used in jostling between rivals. Male king-crickets (Stenopelmatidae) are similarly armed, while many Dynastinid and Scarabaeid beetles have curious spikes and horns protruding from their head and thorax. In each case, such adornments are either totally absent or much less exaggerated in the female.

The primary purpose of sexual differences like these seems clear: the males sport their brilliant colours or strange shapes in order to attract females and, more often than not, their exhibitionism is linked to well defined territories. Dragonflies are particularly territory-conscious, regarding certain stretches

Sexual dimorphism. These male and female common earwigs (*Forficula auricularia*) can easily be distinguished by the shape of their forceps, the male's (bottom) being more curved.

of river or lake as their own and challenging and jostling intruding males of both their own and other species. In their case, however, while there may be considerable differences in colouration between the sexes, it is usually the male that takes the initiative, sallying out from his perch in her pursuit. Male banded agrion damselflies (*Agrion splendens*), on the other hand, indulge in an elaborate female-attracting display, fluttering their storm-cloud-blue-banded wings, perhaps while resting on a lily pad, as a signal to the uniformly dull green female.

Sexual communication of this sort is obviously at least partly visual and is even more significant in groups where colour differences between the sexes are minimal or absent. Male mayflies' eyes are always considerably larger than those of the female and in some groups (e.g. *Cleon*) are divided into two sections, one pair with larger facets geared for greater light absorption, the other with smaller ommatidia enabling recognition of the female at close quarters. Even in highly colourful insects, however, it seems certain that

Mating marbled white butterflies (*Melanargia galathea*). Europe

The mandibles of male Lucanid beetles are often grossly enlarged, not for feeding but for sexual display and jostling with rival males. This is a male *Cyclommatus tarandus* from Mount Kinabalu, Borneo.

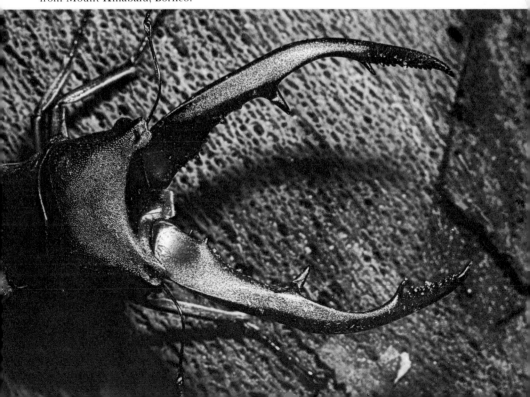

Female moths emit a scent pheromone to attract males at night. This female burnished brass (*Plusia chrysitis*) is resting on her larval food plant – a nettle – and extruding a brush of scent-bearing hairs from the tip of her abdomen.

other stimulants and attractants are involved, notably scent. Male butterflies exude a female-beguiling scent, or pheromone, from special pockets called *androconia*, which may be present on the wings or, in the large Danaids, as brushes on the tip of the abdomen. During Satyrid butterfly courtship, the male actually enfolds the female's antennae with his wings, thus bringing them into direct physical contact with his androconia. Some tropical butterflies shake scent from their abdominal hairs over the female.

Scents like these are clearly designed to work best at close quarters, but others are geared to bringing the sexes together from much greater distances. In this case, it is usually the female that produces the olfactory substance, from special glands at the tip of her abdomen, which may be visibly extruded. A variety of insects dispatch chemical signals of this kind, including butterflies, but the technique is employed to most spectacular effect in their relatives, the moths. Female moths commonly begin to 'call' in this way immediately after emergence from the pupa, usually at dawn or dusk, and may not fly at all until after mating. The effectiveness of the enterprise is increased by the fact that males usually emerge first, so that a virgin female does not have to wait long for an answer to her amorous signalling, especially since her scent, in many cases, can be detected over a very considerable range. Members of the family Saturnidae, or silk-moths, both sexes of which have their forewings and hindwings decorated with startling eye-like markings, present some of the most remarkable instances of the long-distance allure of moth pheromones. In his *Social Life in the Insect World*, the great French entomologist Jean-Henri Fabre vividly describes an evening when his study was literally invaded by several dozen males of the giant emperor or peacock moth (*Saturnia pyri*) – the largest European moth, with a wing span of some 125 mm (5 in) – attracted by a solitary female which had emerged there earlier. Just how far the males had flown on this particular occasion is unrecorded but it is well established that male moths – especially powerful fliers like the Saturnids – commonly travel distances of several miles in response to female scent. Even more remarkable, perhaps, is the fact that they are able to distinguish it from the multitude of other aromas that one would imagine might mask it.

Scent is of particular importance sexually when the female has become so totally adapted for reproduction that she has lost the power of flight. Female Lymantrid moths, such as the common vapourer (*Orgyia antiqua*), have mere stubs of wings, useless for flying, and a plump abdomen that is already full of eggs when she leaves the pupa. The female simply waits until a little rusty-brown male arrives and, after mating, deposits her ova in a neat pattern over her pupal cocoon. Female Psychid moths similarly stay in their larval/pupal cases until visited by a suitor, as do some Chironomid midges, while such a condition is taken to extremes in the little-known *Stylops* (Strepsiptera), the female of which spends her whole life within the abdomen of a bee and is not merely wingless but legless and eyeless too.

A clue to the method by which male insects are able to respond to the scents of the females is gained from comparison of their antennae. Where such communicative means are paramount and the male does the chasing, the latter's antennae are by far the more elaborately developed. Many male moths have the most splendid feather-like antennae, whereas those of the

Silk-moths (Saturniidae) are able to attract males from very considerable distances This female giant Emperor moth (*Saturnia pyri*) is newly emerged and ready to mate. Photographed in Corfu, Greece.

female are much simpler in structure. Elaboration of this sort, presenting a multitude of separate surfaces, enables as many as 40 000 sensory nerve cells, capable of picking up just a few scent molecules, to be concentrated within a relatively small area. Moreover, the antennae are 'tuned' to respond only to the one scent and no other, which is precisely why moths fly so unerringly to potential partners and are not confused by other scents, even when the 'caller' is surrounded by a variety of strong-smelling substances.

It is now well established that a great many insect groups employ pheromones as sexual attractants, among them bark-beetles, lacewings, hanging-flies (Mecoptera), Anthocorid bugs and some 'voiceless' (i.e. non-stridulating) crickets and grasshoppers, in addition to those already mentioned. Perhaps not surprisingly, only a small proportion of such scents are appreciable by the human nose and most of them are produced by butterflies and moths. Some butterfly pheromones are reminiscent of vanilla, chocolate, musk and pineapple; the female lappet moth (*Gastropacha quercifolia*) exudes an odour not unlike that of charcoal or burnt wood, while in male Amathusiid butterflies the male's scent is so persistent that it still clings to specimens which have lain in the collector's cabinet for many years.

If insects' sexual scents are not intended for appreciation by the human nose, then neither are the sounds emitted by a variety of insects for courtship purposes. Indeed, they vary in character from the most subtle to the harshly strident, conducive to nervous irritability. 'Strident' is an appropriate adjective here, since the best known insect musicians are the crickets and grasshoppers, both of which produce their individually characteristic sounds by *stridulation* which involves one part of the body being rubbed or scraped over another. Sun-loving grasshoppers produce their sounds by rubbing the edges of the enlarged femora against hardened edges on the forewings, or tegmina, the legs being moved alternately. In the mainly nocturnal or

Mating weevils (*Elytrocheilus* sp.) in a New Guinea rain forest.

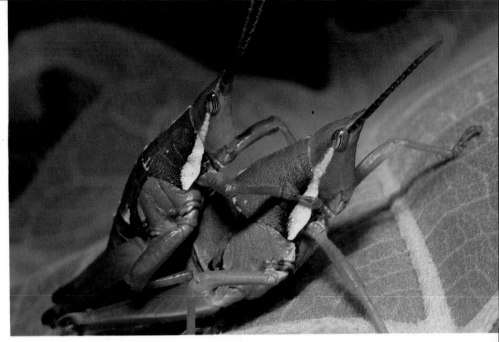

Grasshoppers (*Sphenarium* sp.) mating. Veracruz State, Mexico.

crepuscular crickets and bush-crickets, a somewhat different technique is employed, one tegmen being drawn over another – left over right in true crickets, right over left in bush-crickets. No two species of Orthoptera produce songs that are exactly alike and in some countries with limited faunas, such as Britain, it is perfectly possible to distinguish species purely from their stridulations. Some are pleasing and evocative, like the low whirring call of the European mole-cricket (*Gryllotalpa gryllotalpa*) which, with its short pauses and subtle changes of pitch, has been likened to the call of the equally nocturnal nightjar or the sound of an angler releasing his line. Dickens's 'cricket on the hearth' (*Acheta domesticus*), a cosmopolitan species, produces a cheerful if rather monotonous chirrup, whereas, by contrast, the call of the southern African *Macrogryllus consocius* can have a quite ear-shattering effect, not least because of its large size and the fact that it tends to live sub-socially, in small colonies. Another African species, *Brachytrypes megacephalus*, is said to produce stridulations audible over a distance of more than a kilometre. Even such champions as these, however, would surely be as nothing when compared with an extinct species of Triassic cricket which had a wing span of 300 mm (12 in) and a sound-producing apparatus to match!

A little thought will make it clear that how far a stridulating insect's sounds carry depends to a large extent on what means of amplification it employs. Grasshoppers seem to have no special device for this purpose, the abraded forewings merely vibrating in response to the scraping action of the femora, although in some groups, notably the curious bladder grasshoppers (Pneumoridae) the virtually hollow air-filled body acts as a drum-like resonator, producing a most distinctive range of sounds unlike those of any other Orthopterans. Crickets and bush-crickets have polished mirror-like membranes on their tegmina which act as sound amplifiers, the wings being raised during stridulation to create a space between them and the body. A 'baffle' effect can be produced by varying the height to which the tegmina are raised, making the sound seem to come from far or near, according to the songster's whim. This is why so many crickets, in particular, seem to be excellent ventriloquists and are often exceedingly difficult to locate by means of their song, which seems to come first from one position and then, when you feel you have located it, from quite a different one. Some Orthopterans compensate for the relative weakness of their songs by using vegetation as a resonator. Tree-crickets (*Oecanthus*) use their lair in a silk-bonded leaf as a sound amplifier, varying the pitch of the sound by partly or wholly closing the entrance with their bodies. The European *Meconema thalassinum* goes even

Mole-crickets (*Gryllotalpa*) stridulate by rubbing one tegmen against another, producing a characteristic continuous reeling note. This one is from Trinidad.

further; as it has no means of stridulating, it merely taps a leaf or other suitable substrate with its legs and body, producing a subdued pattering sound which, nevertheless, seems to have the required effect of attracting a partner.

We have mentioned that the calls of different species of grasshopper and cricket vary from one to another, but even the sounds produced by individual species differ according to need. Initial calls may be of a challenging type, simply to let both females and rival males know that the caller is about; once confronted by a female, however, the male may produce a quite different overture of a subtly wooing nature. Nor is it invariably the male who has the monopoly of sound production. In some grasshoppers, e.g

A male cicada (*Cicadetta montana*) feeding from a birch twig. Only males 'sing'. *C. montana* is a European species and is the only cicada found in Britain, where it is extremely rare.

Chorthippus brunneus, the female answers the male with a closely similar song which he, in turn, is able to distinguish from those of rival males.

Those other champion songsters, the cicadas, belong to a quite different insect order (the Homopteran group of the Hemiptera) and their sounds are produced by a very different method, although for much the same reason as in the Orthopterans. In these, the sound-producing mechanism consists of drum-like membranes (called *tymbals*) on each side of the upper part of the male's abdomen, to which are attached internal muscles that alternately contract and relax to distort the tymbals' shape. Each tymbal is operated alternately and the effect is of a series of 'plicks', but speeded up to such a degree that they are not individually distinguishable, at least by the human ear. In principle, the sound-producing method is comparable to the 'clacking-lid' toy, once a favourite of children, in which the alternate pulling and relaxing of a piece of string, passed through a tin lid and knotted on one side, produces a sound. Such an instrument is scarcely musical and, indeed, the same may be said of the songs of many species of cicadas. Some are so loud and penetrating that they have been variously likened to someone banging on a tin, the teeth-gritting screech of a saw cutting into metal, the clanging of a bell and the shrill whistle of a steam-engine. When the males sing in concert, as they frequently do, the overall effect can be almost deafening, attaining a volume of sound that would probably be injurious to the hearing of birds and mammals, including man, if suffered for lengthy periods. In the USA, for example, concerts of these insects were recorded as producing 80–100 decibels at a distance of 18 m (60 ft), the equivalent of a pneumatic hammer or an underground train coming into a station. It is not unlikely that such deafening cacophanies of sound serve a purpose additional to the attraction of the voiceless females, i.e. driving away predatory birds and other enemies. However, by no means all cicadas are as noisy as this. *Cicadetta montana*, which occurs throughout much of Europe, although confined in Britain to Hampshire's New Forest, produces a call which is so 'thin' and high-pitched that it is above the auditory threshold of many people with normal hearing and has been likened to the hiss of gas escaping from a cylinder under exceedingly high pressure. Most of the world's 1500 or so cicada species are found in warmer countries, especially the tropics and Australia, and many of them are very large.

While many insects respond to sounds in a general way via sensory receptors over the surface of the body, specialist singers like the Orthopterans and cicadas naturally require specialised sound-interpretative structures to enable them to separate the calls of their own species from the myriad other noises. Grasshoppers have such 'ears', or tympana, on the sides of the abdomen, while those of crickets and bush-crickets are situated on the tibiae of the forelegs, which are commonly extended in the direction of the stridulation during courtship or the performance of rivals. Both sexes of cicadas have similar sound-receptive membranes.

Various other insects produce sounds which would appear to have sexual

Male 'clicking' or 'cracker' butterflies produce loud clicks in flight by means of a special mechanism on the hind edge of each forewing, perhaps to broadcast territorial claims or as a signal to females. This particularly beautiful species, *Hamadryas arinome anomala*, is feeding from urine-soaked ground in Peru.

significance, although they are rarely as strident as those of the Orthopterans and cicadas. Male *Corixa* (water-boatmen) actually stridulate while under water, which is an excellent conductor of sound, and their song is interpreted by means of tympana, like their more famous Homopteran cousins. Male clicking-butterflies or 'crackers' (*Hamadryas*) of the Neotropics and Australian whistling-moths (*Hecatesia*) can produce sounds by the friction of their wings or the wings and legs in flight and these probably serve as an advertisement of territorial rights as well as a sexual communication; they may also be defensive since they are commonly uttered when man or animals cross their path. In other insects, the sounds produced involve no stridulation but are caused by the callers employing their substrate or other surface for the purpose.

Male death-watch beetles (*Xestobium rufovillosum*) produce a sound like the quiet ticking of a clock by rapping their armoured heads against the sides of the larval tunnels. Some book-lice (Psocoptera) apparently communicate in a similar way. Still more different is the sound stimulation employed by mosquitoes and midges. Here, it is the frequency of the female's wing beats that attracts the male by causing his plumose antennae to vibrate in response, the sound being interpreted by special organs at their bases. The antennae of the male insects are much more elaborately 'feathered' than

Male and female glow-worms (*Lampyris noctiluca*). The female (below) has three bands of luminescent material (*luciferin*) on the tip of her abdomen which produce a beautiful greenish glow when oxidised by the action of enzymes. She is wingless and waits – glowing – until the smaller winged male (above) observes her light with his well-developed eyes. Europe.

those of the females and indeed are basically similar to those of the male moths referred to earlier, except that their role is closer to that of a man-made radio aerial than a chemo-tactile receiver.

Light, as a means of bringing the sexes together after dark, is almost if not quite the sole province of the so-called fireflies and glow-worms belonging to the beetle families Lampyridae, Elateridae and Phengodidae. In the first and best known family, the female is often very much the more luminous of the sexes and is also sometimes wingless, although there are others, such as the southern European *Luciola* and American *Photuris*, where both sexes are equally active and luminescent. The males of the sexually dimorphic *Lampyris noctiluca* (the British 'glow-worm') and the smaller *Phausis splendidula* have much larger eyes than the sedentary, strongly glowing females and these help them to detect their partners as they fly above them. The incandescent area in the female is confined to the last two or three segments of the abdomen but, in the curious South American *Phrixothrix tiemanni*, the worm-like female has eleven pairs of greenish lights arranged along the length of her abdomen, together with a reddish glowing area at the head, and is colloquially called the 'railway worm'. Species of the North American genus *Phengodes* are similarly lit-up, but lack the red headlight. *Pteroptyx* of South-East Asia possesses more conventional lights but employs a most spectacular system of signalling, male answering female, and vice versa, in synchronised fashion, producing a dazzlingly beautiful effect when they gather in large numbers in trees and bushes prior to mating.

Some of the most powerfully luminescent of all fireflies – indeed of all animals – belong to the Neotropical *Pyrophorus*. The 25 mm (1 in) long *Pyrophorus noctilucus* is such a powerful light-producer that it has been used by natives in South America and the West Indies to illuminate their huts, several of the beetles being confined in perforated gourds hung from the ceiling. Unlike other fireflies, it bears three luminescent areas, two of them on the hind margin of the thorax, which emit a greenish yellow light, and another at the base of the abdomen which emits an intermittent reddish flash when the insect is in flight. Like the very similar *Photophorus* of South-East Asia, *Pyrophorus* is allied to the familiar click-beetles (Elateridae).

Needless to say there is much subtle variation in the wavelength at which fireflies and glow-worms produce their light, as well as in the manner in which it is displayed; some species emit a steady glow, others produce pulses or flashes of light. Each has its own idiosyncratic system which is readily interpreted by the opposite sex. The light itself is produced quite without heat and is basically biochemical in origin. It emanates from a usually yellowish-white substance, called *luciferin*, which is oxidised and broken down by means of a special enzyme (*luciferase*), releasing energy in the form of virtually cold light. The process is aided by a crystal layer behind the luciferin which seems to act as a reflector. One of the fascinations of firefly light is that, for sheer physical efficiency, it is superior to any lighting system man has yet been able to devise. What is more, the luciferin seems totally self-renewing and capable of being 're-kindled' at will, although precisely how this is managed is far from clear.

Mating

Even after all these various communicative methods have served their purpose of bringing the sexes together, mating rarely follows immediately. Elaborate displays may be necessary before the female accepts the male's advances and, as in spiders, their communion frequently involves the male in serious risk of his life. In praying mantids, it is not uncommon for the male to succumb to the jaws of the larger and more aggressive female, while, in other insects, males have found it necessary to devise various means of distracting their partners' attention while the essential business of copulation is undertaken. A male mantis approaches his chosen partner with extreme caution, as if half doubting the wisdom of the undertaking, but any inhibitions he may have had are summarily removed when, during or after the passing of his sperm-capsule or *spermatophore* into her body, the female bites off his head and proceeds to devour the rest of his body. Some female crickets and bush-crickets have an equally abrupt way with the opposite sex, although the male *Oecanthus* manages to obviate his peril by offering a pleasant-tasting secretion from a gland on his thorax, which also has the effect of preventing the female from eating his spermatophore. Other males produce a special kind of sperm capsule, one end of which is eaten by the female while the male's seminal fluid enters her body from the other. Male scorpion-flies (Panorpidae) exude a blob of rapidly hardening, proteinous saliva for the female's delectation, while the closely related hanging-flies (Bittacidae) offer their partners captured insects as wedding presents. In some Empid flies, it is rare to come across copulating pairs in which the female is *not* also consuming some small insect, usually a Muscid fly.

While, in most cases, actual copulation involves the insertion of a spermatophore from the male's aedegus into the female's genital aperture, in some primitive groups fertilisation is indirect. Springtails, for example,

Mantids (*Acontista* sp.) mating. Note how much larger the female is than the male.

This female empid fly (*Empis livida*) is eating a leafhopper while mating with a male.

produce spermatophores at random, simply leaving them in positions where the female is likely to find them. Male silverfish (*Lepisma*) deposit their sperm in droplets, without any protective capsule covering, and then induce their partner to take it up. Fleas are among other insects that produce free sperm, although they copulate in the usual manner.

Depending on the group, copulation may take anything from a few minutes to hours, during which time the pair are joined end to end or the male clings to be female's back. In the latter method, the male may possess various means of gaining a better grip on his partner. Male Dytiscid or diving-beetles, for example, have specially enlarged pads on their fore-tarsi, while the curious snow-flies (*Boreus*) use their otherwise useless spine-like wings for holding the female. Some male beetles with especially enlarged mandibles probably use them for partner-gripping, notably the fearsome-looking *Mantichora herculeana* of south and east Africa, which has the distinction of being the largest of the world's tiger-beetles (70 mm or $2\frac{3}{4}$ in). It is possible that male earwigs use their caliper-like cerci for a similar purpose.

Dragonflies and damselflies employ a unique method of copulation and sperm transfer. Pairs may frequently be seen conjoined in flight, with either the male carrying his partner by the head or neck, grasped by his terminal claspers, or the two being linked together in a curious loop. Such a spectacle

Mating in dragonflies is unique among insects as no direct copulation is involved. The male charges a special capsule on his upper abdomen with sperm and the female brings her abdomen around to engage with it. Meanwhile, the male grasps the female by or behind the head. In these common darter dragonflies (*Sympetrum striolatum*), the more handsomely coloured male is above. Gloucestershire, England.

may be initially puzzling but its explanation lies in the fact that the male dragonfly does not use his aedegus for inseminating the female but employs it to charge with sperm a special capsule on the ventral surface of the second segment of his abdomen. He then grasps the female about the head or neck with his claspers while she brings forward her genital aperture near the tip of her abdomen to engage with this special inseminatory armature.

As mentioned previously (p. 86), insect eggs vary considerably in size and shape. So, too, does the female's choice of site for them and this is commonly reflected in the shape of her ovipositor. Some female insects possess the most striking ovipositors which not merely serve to distinguish them from the male and make them immediately recognisable as adults but are characteristic of the group or species to which she belongs. Female bush-crickets display remarkable sword- or sabre-like ovipositors which they use for delicately cutting into the stems of plants in which they deposit their eggs. Snake-flies (*Raphidia*) have the most delicate, needle-like, slightly upcurved ovipositors, which heighten their snake-like appearance when the insects assume their typical 'striking cobra' attitude. The female snake-fly uses her ovipositor to insert eggs beneath the bark of branches of decaying trees, the emergent larvae preying on those of bark-beetles. By contrast, the even more impressive ovipositors of various ichneumon wasps are inserted, with uncanny precision, deep into the actual wood of trees and into the flesh of wood-boring larvae. The large *Rhyssa persuasoria* parasitises larval wood-wasps (Siricidae) by this means, as do the North American *Thalessa*, whose ovipositors attain the quite remarkable length of 150 mm (6 in). Sawflies, which are members of the Hymenoptera and not true flies, gain their common name from the shape of their ovipositor which has a serrated, saw-like edge for laying eggs in leaves and stems, although the device may not always be externally obvious since it is protected by a pair of sheaths. Grasshoppers' ovipositors are generally only fully extruded when inserted in the soil to deposit the oothecae.

Parthenogenesis

While the urge to mate is one of the great driving forces in the insect world, as it is in most animals, there is evidence to suggest that the male of the species may have been something of an afterthought in their evolution. We may surmise this from the fact that the frequently only reluctantly accepted males tend to have a shorter life span than the females and, in some groups, scarcely, if ever, appear on the scene at all. *Parthenogenesis*, or reproduction by means of the unfertilised egg, occurs in a great many insects, from bees, wasps, ants and allied groups to some crickets and moths, as well as most stick-insects and aphids, although it may take different forms. In social bees, it is in a sense deliberately engineered, since the colony-founding queen has a supply of sperm from the short-lived male but is able to use or withhold it according to need. Thus, for the greater part of the time, she allows some of the sperm access to her eggs while they are still in the oviduct, and thus produces only females (workers or new queens); at other times she closes off her sperm-retaining sac (*spermatheca*), preventing fertilisation of the eggs, which consequently produce only males or drones. In other insects, notably stick-insects, males are either extremely rare or non-existent, so that parthenogenesis is obligatory and an almost unending sequence of females is produced, each of them capable of reproduction without mating. It is clear from this that the two forms of parthenogenesis in bees and stick-insects differ widely. In the bees, males that derive from the queen's unfertilised eggs are still able to mate, despite possessing only half the genetic material which results from the fusion of male and female gametes; the 'daughter' females are all potentially fully sexual but only become reproductive queens if fed on an especially nutritious diet. Stick-insects, on the other hand, produce only females, which in turn do likewise.

Parthenogenesis may be the sole method of reproduction in some insects, whereas in others it may alternate with a sexual phase, and often the whole

Female bush-crickets, like this *Neobarrettia vannifera* from Tamaulipas State, Mexico, have very long sword-like ovipositors for laying eggs in vegetation.

cycle involves another short cut to reproduction – *viviparity* or live birth. Such a system is found in gall-wasps (Cynipidae) and also in aphids. The aphids one sees in the height of summer are all females which produce fully formed young parthenogenetically until the end of the season, when both winged females and males are produced. These mate and the females lay eggs which hatch in spring to produce parthenogenetically breeding females.

Aphids produce fully formed young, without mating, for the greater part of the year. Males appear only at the end of the year, mating with females to produce overwintering eggs. In these *Macrosiphum cholodkovski* the large female (centre) has just given birth to live nymphs.

Asexual reproduction, particularly when it is accompanied by the production of fully formed young, has obvious advantages, principally that no time and energy is wasted in seeking mates, and the young can begin to feed and grow straight away and take the fullest advantage of optimum feeding conditions. However, such assets are offset to some extent by the fact that, without the fusion of genetic material from both male and female, more particularly from different populations, there is no opportunity for those variations to arise which are so essential if insects are to adapt to changing conditions. A parthenogenetic female's daughters will contain precisely the same hereditary cell make-up as the mother. Perhaps the main advantage of parthenogenesis for those insect groups that do not use it as their normal method of reproduction is that it makes an excellent stand-by, e.g. if males are in short supply for some reason. Indeed, it is clear that there are very few insects which are *not* capable of reproducing without male help if the need arises.

Paedogenesis

An interesting reproductive phenomenon displayed by some insects is the ability to bear eggs or young before they themselves have attained full adult growth and this is known as *paedogenesis*. It is far from common but is probably best known in the primitive springtails which continue to grow and shed their cuticle with intervals for mating and oviposition. Certain gall-midges (Cecidomyidae) are particularly bizarre in producing very large parthenogenetic eggs which hatch to produce larvae that in turn already contain developing larvae inside them. When these latter emerge from the parent larva they continue to reproduce in exactly the same way until one

This whiskery 'bedeguar gall' or 'Robin's pin-cushion' on wild rose is produced by larvae of a parthenogenetic gall-wasp, *Rhodites rosae*. Europe.

generation pupates to produce either male or female fully adult midges. A somewhat similar method of larval reproduction is displayed by some beetles, such as the North American *Micromalthus debilis*. Aphids and Polyctenid bugs, which live as external parasites of bats, also produce young which have been developing in the female's ovaries for some time before she matures, although this is perhaps not quite true paedogenesis since the progenitors have become fully adult by the time the nymphs emerge.

Polyembryony

The division of a single fertilised egg to produce twins, triplets, quadruplets, or even greater multiples of individuals, is something we tend to think of as primarily a mammalian, and especially human, feature. But some insects have taken this method of reproduction to even greater lengths. It is particularly characteristic of various parasitic Hymenoptera, notably of the families Eucrytidae, Trichogrammatidae and Proctotrupidae. It occurs when a single fertilised egg, laid within the tissues of a host, divides to produce a number of separate embryos (in an almost precisely similar way to that in which identical twins are produced in man) which feed and mature together in this sheltered environment before eventually forcing their way out of the host insect's cuticle. A variety of hosts are attacked in this way. Proctotrupid wasps, for example, commonly parasitise the larvae of rove-beetles and ground-beetles, the wasp's larvae eventually pupating on the outer surface of the host's cuticle like a row of tiny white gargoyles.

Caring for the Young

It is characteristic of most insects that the ovipositing female displays little or no regard for the future welfare of her young, apart perhaps from positioning the ova where they are less likely to be discovered by predators. Once laid, her eggs have no interest for her. In any case, the energy consumed in mating, seeking suitable egg-laying sites and oviposition itself tends to be only just sufficient for these purposes and, more often than not, the female dies soon after these activities are completed. Nevertheless, direct care and protection of the eggs and larvae is by no means unknown in the insect world. It reaches its height in the social bees, wasps, ants and termites, where the nest community is so totally geared to ensuring the survival of the greatest possible number of new adults that a quite separate worker caste of non-breeding females has been evolved, specially 'programmed' to care for the immature stages right up to adulthood. Insects like these arouse much interest, even among non-entomologists, because of their elaborate organis-ation and display of ways of life which appear analogous to our own. Unfortunately, such comparisons are largely spurious. Any concept of affection or love, for example, can safely be said to be outside insects' nature; the selfless care bestowed on the young by worker bees, wasps and ants is distinctly robot-like and if there is any altruism involved it is of the genetic not the moral kind.

The curious thing is that we get rather closer to the human child-parent situation in a number of other rather less well-known, non-socially organised insects, where care of the young devolves on the female alone – the male being only rarely involved. Some such 'single parents' are so selflessly devoted to their progeny that they elicit the admiration of the most pragmatic zoologist. The female earwig, for example, can rarely be induced to leave her batch of some 40–60 eggs during the 2–3 weeks it takes for them to hatch; meanwhile she licks and regularly turns the eggs to prevent possible fungal infection and defends them against intruders to the nest cavity. She also feeds the tiny nymphs on her own saliva and regurgitated food and does her best to shield them with her body. Any disturbance may result in the female carrying eggs or nymphs one by one to an alternative site. Various Heteropterid bugs, notably the little parent-bug (*Elasmucha grisea*), behave in a similar way, while some kind of parental care is also typical of certain beetles and crickets. Adult burying-beetles (Silphidae) feed their larvae, mouth-to-mouth, with liquid food derived from the animal carcases they inter for their benefit. Passalid beetles chew up and partially digest wood for their larvae's consumption and also help them to construct their pupal cocoons. Ambrosia-beetles (Scolytidae) feed their young on the fungus that

This superbly camouflaged praying mantis (*Galepsus* sp.) is standing guard over her equally cryptic egg-batch on dead doum-palm leaves near Mombasa, Kenya.

The common earwig is an extremely solicitous parent, guarding her eggs and feeding her nymphs until they are capable of independent activity.

grows in their tunnels in bark and wood and are also solicitous in removing their faeces. Similar devotion is shown by the American cricket, *Anurogryllus muticus*, as well as by mole-crickets (*Gryllotalpa*) and some cockroaches. The German cockroach (*Blatella germanica*) carries her purse-like ootheca around with her until the eggs hatch, while the soil-dwelling *Panesthia* of Australia exist in family communities of adult males, females and nymphs of varying size.

Female cockroach (*Methana marginalis*) carrying her ootheca or egg cocoon in a Queensland rain forest.

Chapter 10

Social Insects

It is clear that parental care of the kind outlined in Chapter 9 represents the beginnings of true social behaviour and, indeed, it is possible to find almost all stages in its development towards the ultimate condition found in honey-bees and bumble-bees, Vespoid wasps, ants and termites. (It must be emphasised, incidentally, that 'social' in the entomological sense has specific application to those insects which are organised in such a way as to be inter-dependent, show a division of labour, usually with a 'caste' or worker system, and display parental care; it does not extend to those groups which are simply found together in large numbers, such as aphids and caterpillars.)

True insect socialism probably had its beginnings when the colony-founding female occasionally began to live long enough to see her young not only mature but, stimulated by hormonal community-bonding secretions, remain in the nest to care for a second generation. The next step would be for the majority of the females to give up their own egg-laying potential and become mere nurses of the founding queen's eggs and larvae. It is, as we have seen, principally in the Hymenoptera that such a caste system operates but the interesting thing is that such socially organised groups are very much in the minority in the Hymenoptera as a whole – about 5% of an estimated

Leafcutter bee (*Megachile willoughbiella*) cutting a segment of a rose leaf for building her larval nest cells.

Spider-hunting wasps (Pompilidae) paralyse spiders with their sting and then stock a special burrow with them for their larvae's food. This female *Anoplius infuscatus* is dragging an *Alopecosa* spider to its nest in sand-dunes in Wales.

100 000 species. The great majority of bees and wasps are either solitary or semi-social – lacking a worker caste but often giving indications of a progression towards that stage. Leaf-cutter bees (*Megachile*), for example, are among those on the lowest rungs of such development, although they make quite elaborate provisions for their larvae. Sparsely covered with reddish orange hairs, these little blackish bees construct series of tiered cells, initially cut as semi-circular sections from the leaves and petals of roses and other plants, which they stock with nectar-moistened pollen; this is collected by the female on hairs on the underside of her body, not, as in honey- and bumble-bees, in pollen baskets on the legs. Each cell, which looks very like a cigar stub, then receives a single egg and is sealed off and forgotten. Various solitary wasps, such as spider-hunting and potter wasps of the families Pompilidae and Eumenidae, take a similarly limited interest in their larva's progress; provisioning flask-like cells or earthen burrows with still-living spiders and caterpillars, paralysed by the female's sting, for the single larva's consumption. A step towards 'socialism' may be said to have been made when such larval cells are not simply provided with a mass of food and then left but *progressively* provisioned, thus necessitating regular food-gathering sorties on the female's part, just as parent birds bring back food for their fledgelings. This type of parental care is seen in some species of sand-wasps (*Ammophila*), as well as mining-bees of the genus *Halictus*. Sand-wasps, which have reddish, black-tipped abdomens, rather like a bulbous-ended laboratory flask, are of particular interest since they commonly tend a number of burrows, each containing a larva at a different stage of development; only when the larvae pupate does the female consider her work done.

Halictus presents a further step forward towards social conditions. Here, the overwintered female, having mated at the end of the previous summer, lays her eggs; she feeds the larvae when they hatch and survives until, and after, they attain adult form. The old queen continues to lay eggs after her daughters mature and the latter tend the second generation of larvae as if they were their own, constructing their cells and gathering food for them. Later, the queen and some of the 'workers' lay unfertilised eggs, which produce males and these mate with the females, who then hibernate through the winter before starting new colonies the following spring. It should be noted that the queen's daughters are not true workers since they are quite able to breed – unlike those of the true social groups whose workers are generally sterile with atrophied reproductive systems – but it is clearly only a short step towards an even more clear-cut division of labour, such as is found in the bumble- and honey-bees.

Social Bees

Among the most simply organised of the true social bees are the well-known bumble- or humble-bees (Bombidae), which endear themselves to us with their bumbling flight, unaggressive nature and links with the earliest flowers of spring. In fact, bumble-bees are most typical of temperate regions, being much less frequent in the tropics and virtually absent from Africa, Australia and New Zealand. The cells which these bees make for their eggs and larvae are rather untidy affairs, bearing no resemblance to the remarkable individually hexagonal structures created by honey-bees and Vespoid wasps; neither are their nest populations anything like as large, rarely consisting of more than a few hundred workers. Commonly constructed in the ground, perhaps in a vacated mouse- or vole-hole, the nest is started entirely on her own by an overwintered queen. She first makes a ball of wax, secreted by epidermal glands, in which she lays several dozen eggs, sealing them off after provisioning the cell with a mass of pollen and honey (nectar which has undergone chemical change in the queen's crop before regurgitation). Further cells complete with eggs are added at intervals. Pollen is gathered on her hind legs in special pollen baskets, or *corbicula*, consisting of a groove edged with bristly hairs. The queen's nectar-sucking is of particular interest since her proboscis ('tongue') is longer than that of other bees, including honey-bees, enabling her to exploit flowers such as clovers, which are inaccessible to other groups. As soon as the first adults emerge from the eggs – all of them workers – the queen ceases to forage for them and devotes herself entirely to egg-laying; cells for the eggs are constructed by her workers who also gather food for the whole colony. Later in the season, the queen lays unfertilised eggs, which produce males (*drones*) and special eggs which, on hatching, are fed with an enriched diet and become new queens. The drones then mate with the new queens who either leave to found new colonies or hibernate through the winter. In warmer, drier climates, where pollen and nectar may periodically be in short supply, the queens may also undergo what may be called summer or dry-weather diapause (aestivation).

One important difference between bumble-bees and honey- (or hive) bees is that queen honey-bees possess no pollen baskets and therefore cannot gather this protein-rich material which is so essential for the foundation and proper development of the colony. Neither can they produce wax for constructing the egg/larval cells. For both these reasons, queen honey-bees are unable to start new colonies entirely on their own, which is why new queens leaving the nest are invariably accompanied by a host of workers, specialised to help her in the foundation of a new colony. In this respect, the honey-bee resembles the rather more primitive so-called stingless bees, of the sub-family Meliponinae which are unusual in possessing well developed mandibles and are mainly tropical in distribution.

While essentially similar to that of the bumble-bee, the honey-bee's social organisation is based on a far more elaborate nest structure. The larval cells are almost geometrically precise in consisting of a multitude of conjoined

Worker honey-bee (*Apis mellifera*) feeding from a dandelion flower. Note the full pollen basket.

Mutual feeding in honey-bees (*Apis mellifera*). The worker on the left is giving regurgitated food to the worker on the right. The latter has its tongue extended to take the food from the open mandibles of the other worker.

Social wasps (*Polistes instabilis*) on their nest hanging from a small tree in the semi-desert hills of Mexico's Tamaulipas State.

hexagons, the shape best suited for fitting the maximum number into a limited area. As in bumble-bees, the cells are made of wax, which the workers exude in large quantities and knead into the required shape. The greater number of such cells will be for future generations of workers, but especially large cells, usually at the bottom of the comb, are also set aside for future queens and yet others are reserved for drones. At first, all larvae, irrespective of their future role as worker, queen or drone, are fed on the same diet of nectar and pollen as well as a special substance, popularly termed 'royal jelly', which is derived from the workers' pharyngeal glands and is highly nutritious. However, this is merely to get them started, as it were. Later, the diet for each begins to differ. Drone and worker larvae are no longer fed on the enriched diet of royal jelly but have to be content with honey, which, in the case of the worker larvae, seems to result in a degeneration of their ovaries, rendering it impossible for them even to produce male offspring by parthenogenetic means; as a result their future role of nurses and foragers is predetermined. Queen larvae, on the other hand, are fed continually on royal jelly and so become fully fertile. One intriguing question that arises from all this is just how the founding queen and her helper workers decide on the number of new queens and drones required for the foundation of new colonies. After all, while the queen controls the *sex* of the eggs she lays, she must somehow stimulate her workers into constructing the cells of varying sizes, according to the occupants' future castes, and also have some influence on their feeding, which leads to this determination. No-one quite knows how such a balance is reached, but in any case it is not always precise and there are times when too many new queens and drones are produced. In this instance, the drones may really live up to their name, not merely doing no foraging or nest maintenance but even being largely superfluous for mating purposes, and they are consequently ejected from the hive.

While a familiar sight in both town and country, the honey-bee is really a somewhat artificial addition to the insect fauna of temperate countries. In a sense it is almost as much a domesticated animal as the sheep and cow. *Apis mellifera* ultimately has tropical origins and betrays the fact by being usually unable to exist out of doors in countries with prolonged winters. Its honey, as well as that of related species, such as the aggressive giant honey-bee (*Apis dorsata*) of India and Indonesia, is commonly collected from combs in the wild but, in colder climates, colonies would almost invariably be killed by prolonged low temperatures in winter. Even in the sheltered environment of the hive, the colony has to employ various devices to keep itself warm, e.g. by clustering closely together, pattering the feet and vibrating the wings. So effective are such ploys that the temperature within a hive may commonly be some 20–30°C (36–54°F.) above that of the outside air. Even then, it is pretty certain that such domesticated colonies would not survive the winter were it not for the stores of honey which they amass (frequently supplemented by sugars from the bee-keeper) and which provide them with energy and warmth to see them through. The fact that they stubbornly refuse to undergo any proper hibernation is a clear indication of *Apis mellifera*'s exotic origins.

Social Wasps

The life of the typical social wasp community differs in many respects from that of the social bees. In the first place, wasps have no means of transporting pollen in any quantity and their mouthparts are not geared for sucking but for biting and chewing, so that they can only drink openly displayed fluids or bite into juicy fruits. In fact, the greater part of the food taken back to the nest for the larvae consists of various soft-bodied insects, such as caterpillars and aphids, chewed up and regurgitated in liquefied form. Only at the end of the summer, when their protein-craving larvae have all metamorphosed into adults, are wasps at all troublesome to man by spoiling fruits and making our enjoyment of breakfast toast and marmalade somewhat hazardous. At other times, they must be counted among the most important systematic insect predators, especially when one considers that a nest may contain anything from about 5000–10 000 larval cells, most of which could well be used twice or even thrice during the season.

Another Vespoid wasp idiosyncrasy lies in the construction of the larval comb. While built on the same basic hexagonal plan as that of the honeybee, the whole structure is very different in appearance and consists not of wax but of masticated wood pulp, resembling a kind of tough greyish paper. Throughout the summer, one can often see wasps scraping at wooden posts with their serrated mandibles to gain such pulp for enlarging the nest, although, as in bumble-bees and solitary bees, it is started by a single overwintered queen. The nest may be positioned in a hollow tree, in the ground, or rather more disquietingly in the roof or beneath the eaves of a

A worker hornet (*Vespa crabro*), the largest European social wasp, seeking insects as food for its larvae.

house, and is usually begun as a small pedicel to which the queen adds partially enclosed cells in a descending spiral. About ten to twenty cells are constructed, an egg is laid in each and the larvae are fed with insect food chewed into paste-like form. The workers that emerge continue to enlarge the nest until it becomes a large oval structure and, in those species constructing nests open to the weather, a glandular secretion is added to the outer surface which hardens like lacquer to afford waterproofing.

Hornets, which are really no more than large social wasps, nest in a very similar way, although their communities are usually slightly smaller. Some social wasps, including species of *Polistes*, are unusual in that they leave their completed larval cells open to the elements, without a surrounding envelope, the nest usually being suspended from a tree and commonly attaining a huge size. Since these wasps are mainly found in warmer countries, especially the tropics, it is likely that such an arrangement allows greater circulation of cooling air through the nest.

Ants

One basic difference between ants (Formicidae) and other social Hymenoptera, is that the ants have more or less dispensed with flight as an aid to foraging. Worker ants are invariably wingless and even queens and males possess wings only during a short courtship or 'nuptial flight'; the queens subsequently bite or rub them off, resigning themselves to a totally nest-bound, egg-laying existence. The males quickly die once their copulatory duty is done. A mated queen ant receives sufficient sperm from one or two males to last a lifetime of egg-laying, which in some species can be as much as 20 years, during which time she produces several million eggs.

A basically terrestrial group, ants have contrived to colonise almost every kind of ground-floor habitat, although a few extend their home-making up into trees. The large black carpenter-ants (*Camponotus*) hollow out the trunks of conifers into a network of chambers and passages, sometimes also infesting the wooden timbers of houses and causing their collapse. Weaver-ants (*Oecophylla*) of tropical southern Asia, Australia and Africa construct nests of leaves, fastened together with silk produced by their larvae, which are held in position while other ants bring the edges of the leaves together. Even those ants that nest on the ground, such as the mound-building wood-ants (*Formica*), restlessly forage high up in trees in search of caterpillars and sawfly larvae, as well as aphids and scale-insects, which they 'milk' for their sugar-rich honeydew.

While none of the 8000 or so known species of ants is solitary, some of them display a far more primitive and loose organisation than the social bees and wasps. The much-feared driver- or army-ants (Dorylinae) of Africa, Central and South America and India often have no permanent nest but wander restlessly in search of food or when the production of new queens causes the colony to break up. Such stops as they make may last anything

Green tree-ants (*Oecophylla smaragdina*) drawing two leaves together to make a nest.

from days to several months, in order to allow the queen to produce a new batch of eggs, but they are soon on the move again as the demands of the larvae exhaust the food resources around the 'nest' area. Most animals, small and large, avoid these fierce hunters as they advance in vast spreading columns, the centre consisting principally of workers, perhaps carrying larvae and pupae, the large males and females, and the flanks of huge sickle-jawed workers. Advance 'scouts' lay down scent trails for the colony to follow.

Nests of some species of army-ant, notably the American *Eciton*, are really no more than bivouacs, perhaps in a hollow tree, the queen and her brood being enclosed in a cluster of workers linked together by grasping each other's legs in their jaws. Some African *Anomma* army-ants make more permanent nests, with a system of subterranean galleries and chambers. In either case, however, there is a more or less continual need for migration to pastures new since the number of individuals in these essentially carnivorous ant colonies may run into millions – according to one authority sometimes as many as 20 million – and the availability of insect and other small animal prey must be quickly exhausted by their demands.

One should always hesitate to draw analogies between animal and human ways of life; even so it is interesting to compare these restless predatory ants and their primitive unsettled home life with early man, who must also have been a nomadic hunter with a far less permanent home. Indeed, it is possible to extend the analogy by looking at those ants which not merely have a more settled social life but, like man, may be both carnivorous and herbivorous. Probably most more advanced species of ants consume both vegetable and animal food, but some have become specialised agriculturists. Harvester-ants (e.g. *Messor* and *Pheidole*) actually gather seeds, often cultivated grains, and store them in special chambers, the starchy contents being chewed to produce sugars to feed to larvae and other workers. Parasol ants (*Atta*) of the Neotropics cultivate fungi on a mulch of leaves, subsequently feeding on the fungi's fruiting bodies. And, as we have seen, many if not most ants are avid collectors of honeydew from sap-sucking bugs such as aphids, scale-insects and Coccids. For the most part, the ants do no more than visit the feeding colonies of the bugs, taking away such liquid refreshment as they need, but others construct special shelters for their insect providers and actively protect them against marauding predators. Some ants collect aphid eggs or nymphs and take them down into their nests for farming out onto plant roots, thus making it much more convenient to 'milk' them. The European yellow meadow-ant (*Lasius flavus*) is among several species to enjoy such a close relationship with aphids.

Perhaps the most remarkable ant gatherers of honeydew are the famous honeypot-ants, which exist in several genera in Central America, Africa and Australia. Here some of the community's workers perform the highly specialised duty of living honey containers, hanging from the roof of an underground chamber and being fed with honeydew mouth to mouth by returning foragers until their abdomens become grossly distended.

The organisation of a typical ants' nest is quite as elaborate as that of any other social insect, but essentially differs from bees and wasps in that no comb is constructed for the developing larvae. Instead, there are usually separate chambers for eggs, larvae and pupae (the last-mentioned common-ly enclosed in parchment-like cocoons), perhaps heaped together indis-criminately. Another characteristic of ants is that, unlike worker wasps and bees, which differ only in the tasks they undertake, there are commonly extreme differences in the size and structure of the ant workers. Apart from the often considerable disparity in size between sexual forms and workers – the former are generally considerably larger – the workers themselves may be differentiated into various sizes of majors and minors as well as somewhat bigger soldiers, possessing large heads and impressive jaws. In the case of such groups as the harvester-ants, it seems that the excessively large-headed and powerfully jawed workers are thus equipped primarily to crack the seeds they gather. In others, such as the immense 20 mm ($\frac{3}{4}$ in) long *Myrmecia gulosa* (bulldog-ant) of Australia, huge serrated edged jaws as well as a painful sting are more than sufficient to put even human intruders to flight!

Termites

The termites present a further variation on the social organisation displayed by the bees, wasps and ants. They are the only fully social group, apart from the Hymenoptera, and are also far less matriarchal. Each nest contains a queen and also one or more males who are by no means present only on a temporary basis but are honoured members of the community. Moreover, the workers are not simply non-breeding females but may be of either sex and, in some groups, there are no true workers at all, their duties being assumed by the nymphal termites or by so-called *pseudergates* – nymphs which do not normally develop beyond a certain stage.

While by no means related to the ants, there is perhaps some excuse for termites being commonly referred to as 'white ants', since the life styles of the two groups display certain similarities. Like ants, both queen and male are only fully winged during mating, after which the colony-founding female termite sheds her wings and subsequently never leaves the nest. The difference is that the male termites survive and stay to continue to mate with the queen as required, whereas those of ants (and other Hymenoptera) do not, but soon die. Another similarity to ants lies in the considerable variation of form found in many termites' worker castes. Some have powerful jaws for colony defence, and others have reduced mandibles but vast sclerotised heads, which they use to literally block nest entrances when threatened by enemies, among the most frequent of which are, curiously enough, ants. In some termite families, such as the Rhinotermitidae, a very different type of soldier (worker) caste is present. These possess a curious prolongation of the head and mouth into a snout and, when defending the colony, the soldier can

A rock-like nest of termites (*Nasutitermes triodiae*) in Queensland's eucalyptus woodland.

direct through this a mastic fluid capable of incapacitating or immobilising small attackers.

One obvious difference between the family life of termites and that of the other social groups lies in the fact that the young termites are not helpless larvae entirely dependent on the workers but nymphs active from the start. Thus, a typical termite community is even more of 'a hive of activity' than the nest of the honey-bee or ant. Herein lies another termite idiosyncrasy for, if queen or male dies, one or more worker 'supplementary reproductives' may develop full sexual powers and take their place, although this *only* occurs in the absence of king or queen; normally, the non-breeding workers are hormonally inhibited from developing other than along their pre-destined lines.

In some termite communities, the queen attains enormous size, dwarfing king, workers and soldiers. Queen *Macrotermes*, for example, display grossly distended, egg-filled abdomens, rendering them scarcely capable of movement; feeding is effected, mouth-to-mouth, by the workers. Members of this genus and others of the family Termitidae construct nest mounds from soil and saliva which harden into rock-like structures often many metres high which are a particular feature of parts of Africa and Australia. Other more primitive termites construct their nests in dead trees or even in wooden-structured houses, more especially in tropical regions. Still more nest underground or build curious mushroom-like structures complete with element-protecting cap.

As regards diet, termites are predominantly vegetarian or humus-eaters. Some, such as the drywood termites (Kalotermitidae) not merely burrow into wood in constructing their nests but consume this indigestible material as food, aided by intestinal bacteria and flagellates which break down the cellulose into a more digestible form, a symbiotic partnership which is characteristic of most wood-eating insects. Not infrequently, such termites attack libraries, reducing rows of books to mere covers or irretrievably riddling the pages with holes. Termites of the subfamily Macrotermitinae present a further interesting parallel with ants in that, like *Atta*, they subsist at least partly on fungal fruiting bodies cultivated in special 'fungus gardens' in their underground nests. Such activities are of especial interest since at least one species of fungi occurring in termites' nests has been recorded nowhere else. Apparently it has become so specialised that it is unable to survive without the special devotion of these insect farmers.

Chapter 11
Aquatic Insects

Since the very earliest forms of life are thought to have evolved in the sea, one might be excused for believing that those insects living in or on water are among the most primitive or have remained satisfied with such an environment from the start. However, this is by no means so. The numerous inhabitants of fresh waters – lakes, ponds, rivers, streams and canals – *began* by being terrestrial and, like the adaptable opportunists they are, have merely colonised new territory, perhaps as a result of intense competition on land. Clear evidence of this is revealed in the fact that practically all aquatic insects retain certain links with the land, perhaps in requiring atmospheric (as opposed to water-dissolved) oxygen or in spending only part of their lives in water.

Among the most superficially aquatic and numerous insects of freshwater areas are various Heteropterid bugs, such as pond-skaters, water-measurers and water-crickets. Insects like these seldom even get their feet wet since they

A water boatman or backswimmer (*Notonecta* sp.) uses its specially enlarged hind legs as swimming paddles. It is a predator, piercing and sucking its prey by means of its adapted mouthparts.

Water-scorpion (*Nepa cinerea*) showing the prey-capturing forelegs and breathing siphon.

are able to stride or run over the water's surface by using its surface tension, in which they scarcely make a dent. Since all of the bugs' life is spent in this way, they need no special adaptations for an aquatic habitat, apart from an undersurface of water-repellent hairs which prevents immersion in turbulent conditions. Food, usually dead or dying insects fallen onto the water's surface, is seized by means of specially adapted prehensile forelegs which often look like antennae, thus giving the insects a superficially four-legged appearance. Mating, too, takes place on the water's surface, the eggs being laid on floating vegetation, producing nymphs already adapted for surface living. Some semi-aquatic insects are communal in habit, like the tiny bluish grey springtail, *Podura aquatica*, which forms clusters at the edges of still ponds and lakes where it probably feeds on plant detritus and algae. Further out, groups of whirligig beetles (Gyrinidae), their polished cuticles glistening in the sun, gyrate endlessly in search of small surface prey, seizing them, like the bugs, with their forelegs, aided – remarkably – by two pairs of eyes, one of which views life below water and the other above. Whirligigs are surface swimmers rather than walkers and have the second and third pairs of legs flattened like oars and fringed, but other beetles and bugs venture well below the surface. They include the fiercely predatory diving-beetles (Dytiscidae), fully capable of capturing tadpoles and small fish, as well as large black beetles of the family Hydrophilidae, e.g. the great silver water-beetle (*Hydrophilus piceus*). Its bulk and persistent buoyancy (a problem most insects have to counter by constant swimming movements) tend to make *Hydrophilus* a somewhat inefficient swimmer. What is more, like all adult water-beetles, its adaptation to underwater life is only partial since it cannot utilise the oxygen dissolved in the water but needs periodically to come to the surface, where it traps a bubble of air by means of special receptive hairs between the elytra and the abdomen. Water-bugs, such as the water-boatmen, or backswimmers (*Notonecta*), must do the same. Some aquatic bugs have siphon-like tubes at the tip of the abdomen for breaking the water's surface and taking in air. These are the so-called water-stick-insects (*Ranatra*) and water-scorpions (*Nepa*), to which are allied the giant 'toe-biters' (*Lethocerus*) of South America, Australia and Asia.

One interesting feature of adult water beetles and bugs is their possession of fully operative wings, which enable them to fly to and colonise alternative waters should their original home dry up or become polluted; some of them occasionally fly considerable distances from water and are attracted to artificial light. Water-beetle larvae are more fully aquatic, breathing oxygen dissolved in the water by means of gills. This also applies to the larvae of a large number of insect groups whose adults are free-flying and have little or no connection with water except as a place to deposit their eggs. Dragonflies, damselflies, stoneflies, mayflies and alderflies all have nymphs or larvae that breathe by means of gills; these may be constantly rotating along the sides of the body or, in damselfly nymphs, in the form of three leaf-like lamellae at the tip of the abdomen. A subtly different method is used by dragonfly nymphs which draw in and expel water at the end of their abdomen, washing it over internal gills. A more rapid expulsion of the water results in a kind of jet propulsion, which enables the nymph to escape marauding fish. As we have seen elsewhere, dragonfly and damselfly nymphs are total predators, with an extensible mask device for securing prey. Other fully aquatic larvae may be either predatory or herbivorous.

A further adaptation to water is displayed by mosquitoes. The adults lay mats of eggs which float on the water's surface and the larvae breathe oxygen from the atmosphere via a respiratory plate (Anophelinae) or a tubular siphon (Culicinae) which pierces the surface film. Even the pupae breathe in a somewhat similar way, hanging at the surface like tiny commas and extruding a pair of snorkels from the top of the head. Surface respiration of a different kind is effected by the larvae of the chinamark moths (Nymphulinae) which live enclosed in feeding cases on the undersides of water-lily leaves, breathing air filtered from the water by means of tufted tracheal gills.

Since they are so totally dependent on oxygen-bearing water, the more fully aquatic insect larvae – especially caddis, stoneflies, mayflies and alderflies – are sensitive to any de-oxygenation or pollution of their aquatic

This mayfly (*Ephemera danica*) has just emerged from its sub-imaginal cuticle. It will probably live only a short time after mating. England/Europe.

home; it is for this reason that many of them have become adapted, e.g. by their flattened shape or other means of resisting currents, to life in faster flowing and consequently well-oxygenated waters. A few can, however, tolerate highly unfavourable conditions. The blood-worm larvae of Chironomid midges are among the last insects to remain in stagnant, heavily polluted waters, principally because their blood contains haemoglobin. This pigment readily combines with water-dissolved oxygen which can thus be stored for use, enabling the larvae to survive in conditions which would be impossible for ordinary gill-breathers. Haemoglobin is also possessed by various aquatic molluscs and crustaceans, but is otherwise extremely rare in the insect world as a whole.

In view of insects' only partial adaptation to freshwater environments, it is perhaps not surprising to find that their all-conquering march of colonisation has, for the most part, stopped short of the seas. Problems of turbulence, as well as osmotic and salt balance, seem to have proved insurmountable for most insects, although they have been solved by their arthropod relatives, the crabs and lobsters. Even so, a few groups have made a move in this direction, suggesting that, if things ever became difficult on land, many more of them might – given a few million years or so – evolve adaptations to enable them to hold their own in a marine environment. The majority of marine insects are really no more than sea-siders: littoral species of Thysanura (such as *Petrobius*) and springtails, which live on the surface of scummy pools on the shore and are periodically immersed by the tides. Others, such as the lice that afflict both marine and freshwater mammals, can survive long periods of immersion by breathing stored air or air trapped beneath the hosts' body hairs. More truly marine insects include some forty species of wingless bugs (*Halobates*), which manage to live on the surface of seas and lagoons, in some cases hundreds of kilometres from land, apparently subsisting on small dead or dying marine animals and laying their eggs on flotsam, including seabirds' feathers. Most have a tropical or sub-tropical distribution, although one species, *Halobates micans*, occurs in the Atlantic. Some species of Chironomid gnats are also marine; in *Pontomyia natans*, for example, both the wingless adult females and their larvae live immersed in the salt-water lagoons of Samoa in the western Pacific Ocean. As an ancillary to this, it is worth mentioning that some flies of the family Ephydridae complete their development in inland saline waters. One such species (*Ephydra riparia*), living in salt pools in Cheshire, England, has its larvae parasitised by Chalcid wasps (*Urolepsis maritimus*), which are actually able to swim under water in order to lay eggs in their hosts' integument.

Some insects are able to subsist in what might seem even more unlikely liquids. Species of *Drosophila* (fruit-fly) spend their larval existence in vinegar (acetic acid) or in the bubbly froth produced by the nymphs of froghoppers. *Psilopa petrolei*, a member of the Ephydridae family mentioned above, manages to eke out its existence in pools of crude petroleum in the oilfields of California, feeding at least partly on other insects that have fallen into the

A semi-marine bristletail (*Petrobius maritimus*) on a rock above the splash-zone in North Wales.

oil. In tropical regions, many insects, such as caddis and mosquito larvae, contrive to complete a rapid larval development in rain-filled leaves, but some go considerably further and develop within the digestive liquid at the bottom of pitcher-plants. Just how the mosquito larvae manage to combat the effects of these carnivorous plants' digestive enzymes is not altogether clear: perhaps they do so by producing neutralising anti-enzymes of their own. While there, however, they subsist happily on trapped or partially dissolved insects and live in an enclosed protected environment, where their principal enemies are likely to be other larger larvae of their own species.

Chapter 12
Colouration

Insects are among the most variously and brilliantly coloured of all the world's animals, birds not excluded. They exhibit, quite literally, all the colours of the rainbow, with an infinity of subtle shades between, and commonly from precisely the same cause. The tints they display may be due to chemical pigments but are also frequently structural, and result from the angle at which the light rays meet and are refracted by the insect's surface. Commonly, insect colours are due to a combination of both pigments and structure.

An insect's chemical pigments are present either in the cuticle itself or in the tissues below it, and a variety of shades or patterns may be formed by the cuticle being, to a varying degree, transparent. Most pigments are by-products of the digestion of fats and proteins and are essentially waste matter which is not excreted but stored in the cuticular layers in varying concentrations. It is principally from such sources that the different shades of red, orange, yellow and white exhibited by Pierid ('white') butterflies derive. Other colours, such as yellows and greens, have as their ultimate

The colours on the wings of moths and butterflies may be either pigmental or structural, often both, and derive from the arrangement of scales (modified hairs) on the wings. This is a European golden-Y moth (*Autographa jota*).

The colours of many insects are derived from pigments resulting from stored waste products, as in these 'white' (Pierid) *Appias nero figulina* butterflies, drinking by a Malaysian river.

source the green colouring matter (*chlorophyll*) of plants and are a particular feature of many butterfly and moth caterpillars. The various shades of brown and black in the cuticle of such insects as beetles are mainly due to varying concentrations of *melanin*, an amino-acid derivative, darkened or 'tanned' by exposure to the air.

One feature of insects which display solely chemical-based colours is a

The beautiful colour of this emerald moth (*Hemithea aestivaria*) fades with age and after death.

tendency to fade after death, e.g. as set specimens. Emerald moths (Geometrinae), which exhibit varying beautiful shades of green, tend to turn a drab brownish yellow in the cabinet, as do most grasshoppers. Insects displaying predominantly structural or *interference* colours are much less subject to deterioration, which is one reason why the blue Morpho butterflies and also beetles, such as Buprestid or 'jewel' beetles, are not merely popular with collectors but have long been used for decorative purposes and jewellery, both by local peoples and for trade to Western tourists. There are, of course, subtle differences in the means by which the light is refracted to produce the different colours. In blue butterflies, the colouration is less permanent since it is due to layers of overlapping, easily removed scales, which are arranged in such a regular way that they reflect only the blue part of the spectrum. In other butterflies a truly iridescent effect may be produced, as in the European purple emperor (*Apatura iris*). Here, the scales are so arranged on a base of dark pigment (melanin) as to produce a shifting effect of purple or blue. Other insects, such as weevils, owe their magnificent sky blue or metallic green colours to a clothing of fine scaly hairs. The Buprestid beetles mentioned earlier, as well as many ground-beetles (Carabidae), are different again in that the body surface producing the colour is hardened and quite permanent and sculptured into subtly varying shapes that reflect light at different wavelengths – blue, purple, green, bronze, silver and gold. The purple flush on the elytra of the ground-beetle, *Carabus violaceus*, is due to this cause, as are the metallic marks on various butterfly pupae.

The brilliant metallic colours of many Odonata, especially damselflies, derive from the structural arrangement of pigment granules. Pigment in the wings of such species as *Agrion virgo* is similarly distorted by light to produce resplendent shifting effects of green-blue-purple. In some male dragonflies, such as Libellulids, the pale Cambridge blue of the abdomen has a distinctive structural cause since it initially derives from a fine powdery exudation of the epidermal cells, producing an effect like the bloom on a plum: the granules are so small and regularly arranged that they reflect only the pale blue part of the light spectrum and, indeed, often appear almost white.

An interesting feature of some insects lies in their ability to change their colour pattern according to need, rather as do some reptiles, such as the famous chamaeleon. In some cases, this involves alteration of the nature of the cuticular layer beneath the superficial (coloured) one, which may be variably filled with air or water, thus rendering the insect's appearance light or dark. In others, pigment cells in the cuticle may be dispersed or concentrated to produce a darker or paler effect. Pigment concentrated into smaller areas makes the insect appear lighter, while the reverse effect is produced when its granules are scattered. Much of this changeability of appearance is directly linked to light intensity, mantids, for example, being commonly light-coloured during the day and darker as evening approaches.

Such an attribute presumably has a double benefit, both in assisting in camouflage and predation and in absorbing and retaining body heat. Many dragonfly nymphs can also change colour to match their underwater surroundings. At a slightly different level, some cryptic butterflies producing two or more generations a year may exhibit seasonal colour variations to match changes in their surroundings, under the influence of temperature, humidity and light.

Melanin as a colour component of many insects has already been referred to, and there are groups and species which have developed totally black forms, distinct from the typically patterned species. This may be a result of local climatic differences (black being a more efficient retainer of heat) or as an adaptation to industrial pollution. In the much studied peppered moth (*Biston betularia*), for example, it has been clearly demonstrated that melanic forms of the species, matching the soot-blackened trunks of trees in areas of high industry, have a much greater chance of surviving the attentions of insectivorous birds. Originally resulting from gene mutation, the spread of melanic forms in insects like this may also have other survival factors which are less easy to determine.

The complete absence of colouring material, producing white or colour-less insects, is a particular feature of those groups that spend all of their lives underground or in the permanent darkness of caves. It is typical of Diplura (e.g. *Campodea*) as well as the tiny Protura, termites, and many cave-dwelling beetles, cockroaches and crickets.

Finally, it is perhaps worth mentioning that the eyes of many insects are often most beautifully coloured. Those of horse-flies (Tabanidae), for example, are commonly banded with coppery red and green and have a lustrous satin-like sheen, which nevertheless fades after death. Frequently, such colours are both pigmental and structural, the colour effect being caused by the different size of the ommatidia and the curvature of the eye working in combination with inner layers of pigment. Some insects' eyes seem to glow like live embers when they catch the light: an effect caused both by the presence of crystalline layers in the facets and the absence of any screen between them. Such screens are more often present in diurnal insects. Interestingly, the eyes of many nocturnal mammals, such as cats and badgers, glow in a similar way, because of the reflective layer (*tapetum*) behind the retina.

Mimicry

By means which are difficult to explain, a wide variety of insects have evolved appearances which clearly mimic those of other insects armed with a sting or poisons, while remaining harmless in themselves. Hover-flies, bee-flies and bee hawk-moths, as well as clearwing moths of the family Sesiidae, are just a few of those groups which bear varying degrees of similarity to bees or wasps, both in colour pattern and often behaviour. The little European

The colours of many moths, like this marbled carpet moth (*Chloroclysta truncata*) from Europe, consist largely of a dark pigment called melanin.

Insects are generally colourless directly after they have shed their larval/nymphal cuticle and only slowly gain their full colouration as pigments and hardening materials are pumped into the 'skin'. This nearly adult common earwig (*Forficula auricularia*) is recognisable as a male from the curved pincers. Europe.

The colours of this brilliant squash-bug (*Paryphes pontifex*) are both pigmental and structural. The green iridescence along its sides is effected by the dispersal of light from a minutely sculptured surface. The bug is sucking a vine in the Peruvian rain forest.

A wasp-mimic: the hoverfly (*Syrphus ribesii*), feeding from the flowers of St John's-wort (*Hypericum perforatum*). This is a male photographed in Warwickshire, England. Europe.

Mullerian mimicry in action. Both these butterflies come from the Kakamega Forest in Kenya, but belong to quite different families. *Acraea cotikensis* (above) of the family Acraeidae is mimicked by *Mimacraea krausei* (below) of the family Lycaenidae. Both are distasteful. For such mimicry to be of value, it is essential that both model and mimic are active in the same area.

wasp-beetle (*Clytus arietis*), for example, is not merely strikingly bright yellow and black, with wasp-like yellow legs, but imitates the wasp's jerky nervous movements and is often to be seen on wooden fences and gate-posts – just those places commonly visited by wasps in search of wood-pulp for nest construction. Some Ctenuchid moths add to such deception by displaying what seems to be an imitation sting, while, in other insects, the possession of an otherwise harmless ovipositor, coupled with wasp-like colouration, is sufficient to deter both animal predators and inquisitive humans – the large horntail or wood-wasp, *Uroceras gigas*, is a typical example. Sheer bluff of this kind is known as *Batesian mimicry*, after the English naturalist, H.W. Bates (1825–92), who was the first to describe the phenomenon from observations made during his travels in Brazil.

Another type of insect mimicry is of a somewhat different character and is especially characteristic of various butterflies. In this case a number of genuinely poisonous but quite different species may come to share the same 'warning' colour patterns, and thus share immunity from predation. Certain Satyrid butterflies, for example, imitate Danaids, while tropical Ithomiids take Heliconiids as their principal models. There are even some species of swallowtail butterflies that ape others of the same family. The North American pipeline swallowtail (*Battus philenor*) exemplifies the point, being copied in varying degrees by at least four other members of the Papilionidae. To confuse matters still further, it is not uncommon for male and female mimics to take quite different species as their models, presumably as a result of different behaviour patterns, which, in the female, would be especially concerned with oviposition.

A little thought will make it clear that such *Müllerian mimicry* – first described by the German zoologist Fritz Müller in 1879 – confers survival benefit on both model and mimic. Birds and other predators need to learn that brilliantly coloured insects are distasteful, especially where new, inexperienced generations are concerned. If an initial sampling results in that insect's rejection, other insects sharing a similar colour pattern will also be subsequently rejected or ignored, even if they are not of the same species.

One point that needs to be emphasised about insect mimicry is that there is often no very clear division between Batesian and Müllerian forms of it. Batesian mimics, for example, are not invariably harmless, but are often as unpalatable as their Müllerian counterparts. This in itself must obviously have survival value, otherwise random sampling of the mimics – resulting in no ill-effects on the predator – would reduce them considerably. Mimicry also takes various other forms. The predatory Reduviidae family of bugs includes members practising Müllerian mimicry of highly toxic and gregarious African *Lycus* beetles, as well as others whose shapes closely resemble those of their regularly taken prey, enabling them to approach their victims closely without arousing suspicion.

Chapter 13
Defences

Insects, as we have seen, owe their success as a class to a variety of factors, among which are their small size, adaptability to an almost limitless range of habitats and diet, and their fecundity, which allows them to lose practically the whole of a new generation and yet still survive as a species. Insects need to be numerous, for their enemies are numerous as well. From mammals and birds to spiders and, perhaps above all, other insects, a myriad animals regard them as their legitimate prey and wreak such havoc on insect populations as would quite likely be more significant in effect were it not for the many different defences they employ.

As we shall see, avoidance of capture by predators can, in the insect world, take either an active or a passive form and, not infrequently, both. Headlong flight, coupled with a heightened sensitivity to light, is especially typical of nocturnal insects like cockroaches, whose nervous response to sound is also of an exceedingly acute order. Sounds which would be inaudible to our ears send these long-legged commensals scuttling to the safety of the skirting board; moreover, their eyes possess a layer of reflecting crystals which make them alert to the weakest illumination suggestive of danger.

Another means of showing a predator a clean pair of heels has been developed by a variety of otherwise dissimilar and unrelated insects which jump, usually by means of specially enlarged and strengthened hindlegs. Grasshoppers, fleas, flea-beetles and froghoppers are among these insect athletes. A grasshopper's hind femora display a herringbone pattern of tiny muscles, enabling them to leap a good twenty times their own length. Fleas leap, to escape the grooming teeth or paws of their host or to change hosts, in a subtly different fashion. A pad of rubber-like material, called *resilin*, articulates with the upper part of the enlarged hind femur where it joins the abdomen. By bending its legs and exerting pressure on the resilin pad, the flea builds up energy which is suddenly released when the jump is made, adding considerably to its extent. Flea-beetles are, as their name suggests, tiny flea-sized coleopterans with an almost equally impressive jump, which doubtless stands them in good stead when menaced on their food plants by sharp-eyed insectivores like titmice. The much larger froghoppers – plant-sucking bugs of the family Cercopidae – commonly gain greater leverage for their leaps by raising the forepart of the body on their forelegs.

Highly idiosyncratic variations of jumping technique, not involving the legs at all, are displayed by springtails and click-beetles. The former possess a pronged fork device which is doubled beneath the body and held in place by terminal catches when not in use; when released under tension, the fork strikes the substrate with considerable force, sending the springtail spinning high into the air. High-speed photography has shown that the springtail's subsequent fall to the ground is commonly an untidy, sprawling affair. Click-beetles, the adult forms of the notorious wireworms of agriculture, probably use their own highly individual leaping method principally as a means of righting themselves when they fall on their backs after dropping from vegetation, although it may take several attempts to produce the required result. However, since the spring may also be effected while the beetle is in its normal position, it may also have some value in baffling enemies. In the supine position, the click-beetle produces its peculiar

Click-beetles (Elateridae) can jump when they fall on their backs, both as a means of righting themselves and as a startle device against predators. They can also sham death in thanatosis. The peg and sheath mechanism on the beetle's underside, which effects the jump, can be seen on this *Chalcolepidius porcatus* from Trinidad.

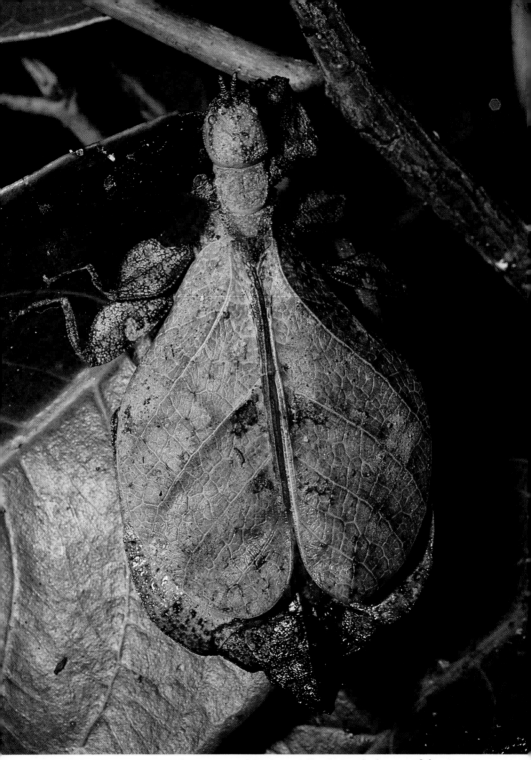

The extraordinary leaf-like leaf-insects (*Phyllium* spp.) live in tropical areas of the Australo-Oriental region. This one is from a New Guinea rain forest.

An exponent of thanatosis or death-feigning: a Brenthid beetle (*Brenthus anchorago*) from Trinidad. Its larvae live in dead trees and timber.

standing-start spring by thrusting the spine which projects from under the hind edge of the first thoracic segment into a special cavity in the next segment, causing an upward arching of head and body in the shape of a shallow V; released under tension, the spine slips out of its restraining cavity, bringing head and body into sharp contact with the underlying surface, thus effecting the leap. Larvae of certain saprophagous flies exhibit yet another variant on the theme of leaping to evade danger. That of the cheese-skipper (*Piophila casei*), which, as its name suggests, feeds on cheese and other dairy products, jumps by bending the whole of its body into a loop, grasping its tail end in its mouth and then releasing its hold after sufficient tension has built up.

Many insects, including the click-beetles already mentioned, display several additional lines of defence, among which is the simple shamming of death or *thanatosis*. When touched or threatened, the beetle draws in its legs close to its body and lets itself fall to the ground, where it lies still for a while until danger is past. Leaf-insects, stick-insects and Brenthid beetles, all of them inanimate-looking enough in the first place, commonly react in this way, as do weevils, lacewings and various moths and their larvae. Many moth caterpillars are common exponents of this ploy, which, in groups like tiger-moths (Arctiidae), is rendered doubly effective by a mass of bristly hairs. Otherwise, thanatosis is probably only variably effective as a predator-deterrent, principally in effecting the potential victim's sudden disappearance or apparent expiry. Certainly, many predatory animals, such as toads, will only take obviously living and moving prey, but there are many other insect-eaters which tend to be far less fastidious in this respect.

An ability to look like part of the scenery, especially vegetation and bark, is a passive defensive technique which has been developed to an amazingly effective and varied degree in the insect world. Mention has already been made of stick-insects and leaf-insects. Some of the latter, such as the Asian *Phyllium*, are so like flat bunches of leaves that herbivores occasionally take a bite at them. The same is probably true of various tropical bush-crickets whose green or brown forewings are not merely leaf-like, complete with veins, but even bear tiny irregular patches and imperfections suggestive of a caterpillar's nibblings. Certain Flatid bugs achieve their disguise by being coloured according to the stage of their host plant's development, some individuals being green like buds, others pink to match semi-developed flowers.

Such *cryptic camouflage* is the particular province of caterpillars of Geometrid moths, many of which are so remarkably like twigs, both in form and colour, that it takes a practised eye to spot them and doubtless also deceives sharp-eyed, colour-perceptive birds. Some caterpillars of this type bear tiny tubercles suggestive of leaf-buds on their body, while in some cases, as in the brown or green larvae of the peppered moth (*Biston betularia*), the bifurcated head is extraordinarily bud-like, too. Such larvae enhance their vegetable appearance by moving and feeding mostly at night and, during

A beautiful leaf-mimic: a species of *Phyllophora* bush-cricket from a New Guinea rain forest.

the day, commonly cling at a twig-like angle to their perch by means of the two pairs of hind claspers. Should they be discovered, many such larvae have yet another trick up their sleeve, which is to drop to the ground supported by a silken life-line exuded from oral glands; when the coast is clear they make their way up again, re-ingesting their 'rope' as they go. Membracid bugs are among other insects practising the art of seeming to be what they are not. Some of them bear highly convincing thorn-like protrusions on the thorax and others have even more bizarre appendages in the form of multiple spines and flanges. The caterpillars of some moths, as well as certain weevils (*Cionus*), look extraordinarily like bird-droppings, while many moths have their wings patterned like bark, frequently with a suggestion of lichen growth.

As in so many forms of insect defence, crypsis is commonly only a first line of defence, to be followed, if it fails, by others of startling effect. Red and blue underwing moths (*Catocala*) spend the daytime clinging to tree trunks with their dark bark-like wings folded down over the body. Any disturbance, however, induces them to display brilliantly coloured underwings – red or blue with a contrasting black band – which may either cause the attacker to leave them alone or confuse it for a long enough to allow the moths to fly a brief distance, settle and 'disappear' once more. Presumably a similar happy effect is obtained by certain otherwise cryptically patterned grasshoppers (*Oedipoda*) which display handsome blue or red wings during their short bursts of half flight, half jump. In some moths, such as the European eyed

Incredible crypsis: the larva of a Geometrid moth (*Eucyclodes* sp.) in a Queensland rain forest.

A typical looper, inch-worm or measuring-worm: the cryptically shaped and camouflaged caterpillar of the peppered moth (*Biston betularia*). Note the bud-like head and body tubercles. England/Europe.

hawk (*Smerinthus ocellata*) and the American bullseye (*Automeris io*), the underwing pattern is in the form of a pair of highly convincing eyes, made up of a pattern of contrasting colours. Some butterflies are similarly patterned but, in their case, it is more usual for the whole of the upper surface of both pairs of wings to be brightly coloured, the under surfaces being cryptically patterned and in some cases – especially the famous leaf butterflies of India (*Kallima*) – presenting an amazingly leaf-like appearance when the wings are closed. A number of butterflies, however, present a variation on the eye-pattern theme by being so adorned on the outer surface of the closed wings. Some of the Brassolids (*Caligo*) of South America bear such strikingly large, staring eyes as to earn them the popular name of 'owl butterflies' – an epithet which seems doubly appropriate in view of the fact that they tend to be most active at dusk. Apart from scaring off predators it is possible that patterns of this sort may benefit their owners in other ways, e.g. by diverting a pecking beak to a less vulnerable part of the body, giving time to make good an escape.

Insects spend a great deal of time preying on each other but, since birds are not overly discriminating in their choice of victims, we cannot be surprised to find that many predatory insects also exhibit bird-deterring patterns. In addition to a variety of cryptically coloured species, some mantids display eye-like markings on their tegmina, which they raise and vibrate when under threat, raising their barbed forelegs in approved praying (or 'preying') fashion for good measure. Since the spined legs of larger mantids can cause quite severe gashes on the skin, the cumulative effect of appearance and armaments is probably enough to occasionally prompt smaller and less ravenous birds to leave the mantid alone and seek more placidly disposed prey.

In many insects, a display of brilliant colours is a clear indication of unpalatability, even of genuine poisonousness. A large number of butterflies and moths are among those many insects which are toxic, both as adults and larvae, and are consequently strictly avoided by birds and other predators. They include the milkweed (*Danaus plexippus*), which as a larva gains its poisons directly from its milkweed food plants, and the magnificent *Parides* and *Troides* birdwing butterflies of New Guinea and Australasia, commonly called poison-eaters from their habit of feeding on *Aristolochia* vines. Zygaenid (burnet) moths, Lycid beetles, certain froghoppers and nymphal and adult grasshoppers (including locusts) are among other highly distasteful insects. Their toxicity may lie stored in the tissues or in the blood, which in some groups is actually voided from the mouth or leg joints in what is known as *reflex bleeding*. African *Phymateus* grasshoppers (Pyrgomorphidae), oil-beetles (Meloidae), ladybirds and leaf-beetles, and many others, react to interference in this manner. In the European bloody-nosed beetle (*Timarcha tenebricosa*), the exuded haemolymph is very like human blood in appearance and, while harmless on the skin, is doubtlessly unpleasant to taste. That of the famous blister-beetle or 'Spanish fly' (*Lytta vesicatoria*) is, however, more directly corrosive in effect and, synthesised as *cantharidin*, has actually been used as a medicinal vesicant as well as a supposed aphrodisiac. Some warningly patterned (*aposematic*) insects aggregate in large numbers, thus, as it were, emphasising the dangers of sampling them, an effect often heightened by their characteristic smell. Such ploys do not always work, however. When supplies of the orange and black cinnabar moth larvae (*Callimorpha jacobaeae*) were exported to New Zealand in an attempt to

While closely resembling thorns, the spiky appearance of these 'thornbugs' (*Umbonia spinosa*) from the rain forest of Peru are probably less cryptic in character than simple physical defences against being swallowed by birds and other small animals.

No better exponent of cryptic camouflage could be found than this superbly camouflaged oak beauty moth (*Biston strataria*) resting on a tree trunk. England/Europe.

The cryptically marked waved umber moth (*Menophra abruptaria*).

The contrasting eyes on the undersides of the wings of this 'owl' butterfly (*Caligo teucer insulanus*) are seen to particularly striking effect at dusk and the early morning when it is most active. It is possible that birds, lizards and other animals mistake these butterflies for predatory owls. This one was photographed in dense forest in Trinidad.

control rampant ragwort plants, local birds eagerly ate them, whereas their European counterparts always tend to give the caterpillars a wide berth. In this case, it is possible that the caterpillars are rather less toxic than their colouration suggests. Their food plant, *Senecio jacobaea*, certainly contains alkaloid poisons but it is possible that the larvae do not retain enough of it to cause a predator serious digestive problems. The handsome black and red adult moths, on the other hand, may well be more toxic.

Patterns of black and red, or more usually black and yellow, are typically displayed by those insects possessing a sting – always females since this primarily defensive weapon is actually a modified ovipositor or egg-laying device. Yellow-jacket wasps and hornets (Vespidae), honey-bees and bumble-bees, as well as ants, are among the mainly social insects thus armed, their poisons being principally mixtures of proteins, enzymes or formic acid. Often the sting is used in conjunction with powerful biting jaws, notably in the fearsome bulldog ants (*Myrmecia*) of Australia and South Africa, whose size, armaments and numbers make them formidable disrupters of many a picnic. In some ants, there is no sting at all, formic acid being literally squirted from the abdomen, as in the mound-building wood ants (*Formica rufa*). Larvae of certain Notodontid ('prominent') moths can also eject formic acid from a gland in the thorax. Many bugs and beetles have a somewhat offensive smell as a result of the possession of so-called stink-glands, and some are able to eject noxious fluids for several centimetres. The Asian Pentatomid bug, *Tessaratoma papillosa*, can do this, as can the snail-feeding ground-beetle, *Cychrus caraboides*. The latter is on record as having temporarily blinded an over-zealous entomologist by discharging irritant liquid straight into his eye! Some termites, as well as primitive proturans, are also able to spray liquids at attackers, although in their case the fluid is of a sticky nature and designed to hamper the aggressors' movements.

Probably the most famous exuders of defensive substances are ground-beetles of the genus *Brachinus*, typified by the 7–10 mm ($\frac{1}{4}$–$\frac{1}{5}$ in) bombardier beetle (*Brachinus crepitans*). Here the reaction to danger is in the form of what is quite literally an explosion, resulting in a small puff of vapour, exuded from pygidial glands at the beetle's tail. Just how the bombardier manages to conduct its cannonade without blowing itself up is not entirely clear, but the beetle is able to produce several salvoes in rapid succession by the interaction of hydroquinones and hydrogen peroxide, which builds up intense gaseous pressure and forces out the corrosive vapour – to the accompaniment of a distinct 'crack'. Certain tiny rove-beetles (*Stenus*) possess a similar explosive device, but without any audible sound. Semi-aquatic in habit, they probably use it for defence and can also propel themselves over the water's surface by what is, in effect, a form of genuine jet propulsion.

Just how often the more densely hairy caterpillars of various moths and butterflies are sampled by birds is difficult to ascertain, but it is likely that they cause considerable discomfort through irritation of the membranes of the mouth. Some such larvae are so coloured and patterned as to deter such

The extreme hairiness of these communally feeding tent caterpillars (*Malacosoma californicum*) from Utah, USA, renders them immune to the attacks of most birds.

These brilliantly coloured hawk-moth larvae (*Pseudosphinx tetrio*) in the Peruvian rain forest exhibit their patterns to warn predators of their distastefulness.

sampling, while others are merely bristly. Lymantrid moth caterpillars, as well as the larvae of Dermestid beetles, possess tufts of erectile bristly hairs which break off readily and cause irritation of tender human skins. Often these and other body hairs contain toxic substances which are released when broken and are capable of inducing varying degrees of urticaria, especially if transferred to the face and about the eyes. Some 'slug' caterpillars of the moth family Limacodidae are especially well armed in this respect, e.g. the North American saddleback larva (*Sibene stimulaea*) bears a battery of stinging rosettes on its sides and upper surfaces which can have a severe nettle-like effect on the skin. In some such groups, the pupal cocoon is festooned with the larva's shed hairs, while the egg batch may be similarly protected by hairs discarded from the female's abdomen.

In many insects, some protection against smaller predators is afforded by a hard cuticle, which may be rendered even more effective as a deterrent if adorned with chitinised spines and 'horns', as in various beetles. Mammals with strong crunching teeth are unlikely to find such devices a serious obstacle, but small insectivorous birds might well experience difficulty in swallowing such beetles whole. Some cockroaches, apart from emitting nauseous odours, roll into a ball and tuck in their legs, like pill woodlice, so that their predators can gain no purchase on them. Female and larval scale-insects lead their sedentary sucking lives enclosed in hardened waxy scales, which serve both to protect them against predatory insects and to maintain their own microclimate. Indeed, it is clear that the homes of many insects are designed for more than one purpose, protecting the occupant not only from the attacks of predators but also from the vagaries of climate and other environmental factors. Caddis larvae of the family Molannidae make cases which are not portable, as in related groups, but fixed to the river's substrate to prevent their being washed away by the current. The froth produced by the larvae of froghoppers prevents their desiccation by sun and wind as much as it does the intrusion of enemies. The vast rock-like nests of certain termites, such as the compass termites (*Omitermes meridionalis*) of Australia, are not merely proof against the most determined predator, or even charges of dynamite, but seem carefully positioned in such a way as to prevent over-heating. There is, moreover, an internal tunnel system, designed to maintain an equable temperature by means of a constant circulation of air.

As we saw earlier, when describing the often literally deafening choruses produced by courting cicadas, it is likely that the sounds emitted by a variety of insects have some value as predator-deterrents. In the cicadas' case, the effect is clearly secondary but in others it is not always easy to say whether the sounds are primarily defensive or sexual. The stridulatory emanations of many Heteropterid bugs, especially aquatic species, could well serve either purpose since it is commonly the case that both sexes can produce sounds. Those of tiger-moths (Arctiidae), on the other hand, seem clearly designed for the sole purpose of warding off the attacks of bats. The moths emit ultrasonic squeaks from special vesicles on each side of the thorax which the bats interpret as a signal indicating their potential prey's unpalatability and as a result do not follow through their initial interest. On the few occasions that bats have been observed to swallow Arctiid moths they invariably disgorged them immediately afterwards – not surprisingly since the moths contain histamines, alkaloids and cardenolide heart poisons, which could well have a serious effect on a small mammal. During the day, of course, the moths' gaudy colouration doubtless serves as sufficient warning for day-active birds and other animals to leave them alone. Some other moths do not seem to produce sounds themselves but, by means of special tympana designed to interpret the bats' echo-location calls, receive sufficient warning to take evasive action.

Certain caddis larvae and cockroaches, as well as the larvae of Scarabaeid and Lucanid beetles, can also produce sounds, basically by means of some form of stridulation – one part of the body being rubbed or grated against

Despite being severely pecked by a bird, this caterpillar of a bright-line brown-eye moth (*Diateraxia oleracea*) moth pupated and produced a perfect moth.

another. In the beetles' case, it is possible that the sounds prevent larvae from crossing each other's path; one would think it would merely serve to *attract* predators!

One question that it is reasonable to ask is: how often, if at all, do insects survive the semi-successful sampling attacks of birds and other predators that must often take place? It is not uncommon, for example, to see butterflies with V-shaped pieces removed from their wings, indicating pecking and either rejection or the insects' subsequent escape. Such mutilation does not usually inhibit activity to any great extent, but the loss of a complete wing or several legs can be a serious matter for adult insects since they are quite unable to replace them. Such is not invariably the case with larvae or nymphs, however. A caterpillar severely pecked and then released by a bird may still complete its development, provided that the forepart of the body is undamaged, since the hormones influencing and dictating metamorphosis are located in the head and thorax. Nymphal stick-insects, grasshoppers and bush-crickets which lose an antenna or leg may produce a replacement at their next ecdysis, the only drawback being that it is usually smaller and indeed will probably never attain its proper size, even when the insect becomes adult. Insects' matter-of-fact approach to life is indicated in the readiness with which some carnivorous species consume their own severed limbs, if they happen to be to hand as it were. The author has actually witnessed this in a nymphal bush-cricket (*Leptophyes punctatissima*) which calmly seized its severed appendage and proceeded to chew up every scrap of it, from femur to claws – a clear indication, if one were needed, that little or nothing goes to waste in nature.

Chapter 14
Migration

An ability to fly over very considerable distances is often as vital to insects as it is to migratory birds. Displaying powers of endurance that are at least the equal of any swallow, insects' peregrinations may take them thousands of miles from their place of birth, frequently in numbers that defy counting. As in birds, the reasons that trigger off such mass movements are usually climatic or pressure of numbers, both of which result in a lack of food, and the movements may be strictly seasonal or more irregular in occurrence. Not infrequently, individual insects make both outward and return journeys, just as birds do, although more often these adults die after reproducing at their destination and it is their progeny that make the return trip to their country of origin.

Of the wide variety of insects that regularly migrate, butterflies are by far the best known, at least in appearance. Western Europeans admiring the brilliant red admirals (*Vanessa atalanta*), painted ladies (*Vanessa cardui*) and clouded yellows (*Colias croceus*) that visit their garden buddleia in summer

A well known migrant butterfly, the red admiral (*Vanessa atalanta*).

may not always be aware that these hardy butterflies, or their parents, have travelled from as far afield as North Africa. As soon as dusk falls, they give way to the moth night-shift, some of which may have arrived from equally long distances, e.g. death's-head, convolvulus and striped hawk-moths, all of them sturdily built with powerful wings, rendering them well equipped for sustained flight. Moths such as these are only spasmodic visitors to Britain and western Europe but others are much commoner immigrants and of such small size as to render their regular arrival a cause for even greater admiration. The whirring, long-tongued silver-Y moth (*Plusia gamma*), distinctive for the clear Greek letter γ on its greyish forewings, arrives in Britain every year in vast numbers from North Africa and southern Europe, despite its wing span of less than 50 mm (2 in). More remarkable still are the migratory movements of the tiny diamond-backed moth (*Plutella maculipennis*), a mere 25 mm (1 in) across the wings and of delicate build to match, which periodically flies across to Britain from Europe via the turbulent North Sea and is believed to undertake similar movements across the Mediterranean, as well as in the USA.

A famous migrant: the monarch or milkweed butterfly (*Danaus plexippus*) feeding among flowers in Oaxaca State, Mexico.

Most migration routes are fairly clear-cut, but some butterflies are such restless wanderers that they have spread their domain far beyond what would seem to be required for the breeding of new generations. The painted lady mentioned earlier is undoubtedly the leading example of this insect search for *Lebensraum* and is almost certainly the most widely distributed butterfly in the world. Its original home is probably North Africa but extended migratory movements have led to its establishment in every continent except South America. Rather less widespread, but no less spectacular in its movements, is the large monarch or milkweed butterfly (*Danaus plexippus*). The migration of this handsome ruddy brown, black-striped butterfly within its native American homeland is remarkable enough – flying from north to central America in autumn and returning north in spring, the insects gather en route in vast communal sleep-ins, suspended from trees and the roofs of caves. This apart, the powerfully flying monarch has now established permanent settlements in places as far afield as the Azores, the Canary Islands, Indonesia, New Guinea, Australia and New Zealand. Occasional individuals turn up in Britain, more particularly in the west, the Isles of Scilly and the Channel Islands, although they rarely breed.

Butterflies like these command admiration and respect, both for their handsome appearance and staying power, while others may be viewed with some suspicion. It is not generally realised, for example, that the large and small white butterflies (*Pieris brassicae* and *P. rapae*) have their numbers supplemented each year by regular immigration. In fact, some sixty species of 'white' butterfly (Pieridae) migrate in various parts of the world but only a small proportion of them are of economic importance. One of them, the American *Phoebis eubele*, is of particular interest in that it appears to be one of the few butterflies, if not the only one, to migrate away from the tropics, from South America northwards to the southern USA.

The migratory movements of insects are in general much less frequently remarked upon (except by entomologists) than those of birds and mammals, but some simply cannot be ignored. Locusts, for example, are really no more than large grasshoppers but the devastation they cause to agriculture leaves the feeding effects of their smaller cousins far behind. Once a locust population is on the move (flying adults, as well as terrestrial 'hoppers'), almost nothing that is green or growing escapes their jaws, including, needless to say, cultivated crops. Many species of locust regularly migrate and, in so doing, cause damage to plantings, but the most economically important of them is the desert locust (*Schistocerca gregaria*), which was probably the species recorded in the Bible (Book of Exodus) as the eighth plague that struck Egypt. It occurs over a great part of north and central Africa, in Iran, Bangladesh and India, extending to Turkey and even southern Europe and, in its normal so-called solitary phase, causes few problems. Paradoxically, it is initially good feeding – not the lack of it – that prompts mass movement and consequent problems for man. Plentiful lush greenstuff in the locusts' residential area, commonly about a river delta, naturally increases nymphal growth and stimulates further breeding, and this in turn brings an increased need for sustenance, as well as neurophysiological stress and restlessness caused by overcrowding and jostling. It is then that the whole colony begins to move, led by the airborne adults, with the as yet flightless nymphs running and hopping in their wake and following them in the air as they mature. The nymphs are more brightly coloured than the

Like several other species, the migratory locust (*Locusta migratoria*) often migrates for considerable distances and may cause much damage to crops. This specimen was photographed in France.

adults, probably partly to deter predation by birds, with darker areas to absorb heat and thus increase their metabolism and therefore their rate of growth. An interesting feature of migrating locusts is that the adults tend to have longer wings than those of the sedentary (solitary) form and, while not among the masters of insect flight, can nevertheless travel for many hundreds of miles, partly because of an ability to lock their wings and glide without excessive expenditure of energy; locusts are also able to survive without feeding for considerable periods, subsisting on stored fats which supply more energy, weight for weight, than other foods. The migrators' instinctive movement is towards areas of low pressure where rain stimulates plant growth, the direction of moisture-laden winds being assessed by sensitive hairs on the upper part of the head. In any case, the locusts are very much at the mercy of the prevailing winds, being carried willy-nilly to fronts where airflows converge, produce rain and, consequently, the right conditions for the travellers to settle and feed.

The desert locust breeds at such a rate when conditions are in its favour that its numbers are frequently calculated more in billions than millions, and the consequences of these myriad chewing jaws on plants under cultivation can prove quite disastrous. Even today, despite insecticide spraying and the more accurate pinpointing of locust outbreak areas, *Schistocerca gregaria* presents probably the greatest problem of insect control in Africa.

Of other species of locusts that can, at times, be almost equally as damaging as the desert locust, the most famous is the so-called migratory locust (*Locusta migratoria*), somewhat misleadingly named since most species migrate to a greater or lesser extent. This, the locust of school and college laboratories, occurs in the form of races or subspecies in Africa, southern Asia, the East Indies, Australia and New Zealand. It also has a regular breeding ground around the north-west coast of the Black Sea and it is possibly from here that occasional stragglers, even small swarms, make their way to western Europe and Britain – a wasted journey since neither they nor specimens escaped from captivity are capable of breeding in such areas or of doing any appreciable damage.

In southern Africa, two of the most damaging locust species are the brown locust (*Locusta pardalina*) and the red locust (*Nomadacris septemfasciata*), the latter being particularly large. Australia has a number of variably trouble-some species, including *Chortoicetes terminifera*, outbreaks of which have been made more difficult to control because of extensive forest clearance. *Schistocerca paranensis* wanders over a considerable area of Central and South America, while North America's most economically important species is the Rocky Mountain locust (*Melanoplus spretus*).

The powerful, purposeful flight of the larger dragonflies has already been referred to at some length in Chapter 4. Their migratory flights are less frequently observed than those of butterflies and locusts but are scarcely less impressive, not least because many people still tend to regard them with a certain amount of suspicion, in spite of their inability to sting. Even aggregations of quite small species can cause considerable popular alarm. In 1947, for example, much local disquiet was expressed by those local people who witnessed several irruptions of *Sympetrum striolatum* – a restless if relatively diminutive dragonfly wanderer – which came in from the sea along the southern coast of Ireland in such numbers as to appear like thick, black clouds. Quite frequently, dragonflies have been observed following the same migratory routes as birds and butterflies, occasionally ambushing and preying on the latter as they go! The Odonata can even boast a globetrotter comparable in performance to the butterflies referred to earlier. The powerfully flying *Pantala flavescens* – one of the Libellulid or darter dragonflies – now occurs virtually worldwide as a direct result of migratory flight. By contrast, most of the dragonflies' smaller relatives, the damselflies (Zygoptera), are far more sedentary in their habits, although a few make relatively modest seasonal movements.

Some groups of flies are regular migrators. Hover-flies (Syrphidae) are not merely masters of the art of aerial acrobatics but are capable of flying hundreds of kilometres across land and sea. Some of these, such as *Syrphus balteatus* and *S. pyrastri*, periodically fly in huge swarms to England from southern Europe and there are regular southward movements in autumn on the Continent. Like ladybirds, which are also frequent infiltrators and are sometimes seen in uncountable numbers around coasts or even floating on the sea, their immigrations can only be welcomed, since the larvae of both are valuable predators of plant-sucking aphids and scale-insects.

Aphids themselves may undertake their own form of migration, if on a more modest local scale. *Alates* (winged sexual forms), after climbing some suitable eminence and allowing themselves to be wafted aloft, may be carried several miles by winds. It is unlikely, however, that they could manage such distances by unaided flight any more than the tiny fringe-winged thrips, millions of which are borne aloft by thermals in hot weather and form much of the aerial plankton eagerly sought after by insectivorous birds. Many other tiny insects, such as certain Psocoptera (bark-lice), effect their dispersal in a similar way. Small plant-bugs and leafhoppers undertake more purposeful migrations, yet they too must be very much at the mercy of the slightest vagaries of wind and weather.

Mass movements may also take place among wholly terrestrial insects, such as army ants (Dorylinae). One particularly huge colony of these restless predators is said to have marched on the Brazilian town of Gioania in 1973 and, in their hunger, eaten several people, including the chief of police! Even rivers may present no obstacle to the ants' relentless progress but are crossed by the simple expedient of forming linked chains with their own bodies.

Ground migrators of another sort include the caterpillars of various moths, which concertedly move to pastures new when their original food supply runs short. European processionary moths (*Thaumetopoea*) normally live in communal webs in oak and pine leafage, but periodically leave their original pabulum to follow one another nose-to-tail in a continuous wriggling column until they find a suitable alternative feeding site. The North American 'army worm' caterpillars of the Noctuid *Leucania unipuncta* justify their name by travelling in military-type units, systematically consuming vegetation in their path. Larvae of certain European and North American Mycetophilid flies (*Sciara*) are popularly called 'snake-worms' because of their peculiar and puzzling habit of making periodic migrations in the form of close-packed columns resembling an undulating serpent in shape.

At the beginning of this chapter, reference was made to the reasons which trigger off insects' mass movements. In many cases, the motivation is clear enough; in others more obscure, less definable factors would seem to be involved, notably where feeding and breeding conditions would seem perfectly adequate to support a virtually unlimited population expansion. If, however, we take the principal factors prompting such movements to be concerned with changes of climate, the need for greater quantities of food and, perhaps, an avoidance of excessive in-breeding, then such criteria might well be applied to insects not often thought of as true migrators, such as ectoparasites. Even the fleas that leap from one sickly, dying or dead host to another healthy one are 'migrating' – and for all the reasons mentioned!

Chapter 15
Insects and Man

It is perhaps not altogether surprising that insects in general tend to present a rather poor image to the public gaze. The entomologist may protest (rightly) that only a very small proportion of the class are at all troublesome to man, but the problem is that the concerted activities of that minority of species can cause immense inconvenience, or worse, thus colouring popular attitudes to the whole. (The same might be said of delinquent youth!) Apart from the mere irritation resulting from their bites, it is pretty well established that more deaths have been caused by such insects as mosquitoes, fleas, lice, and tsetse flies, carrying the micro-organisms that transmit malaria, yellow fever,

Destroyer of many an old building's timber superstructure: larvae of the death-watch beetle (*Xestobium rufovillosum*).

bubonic plague, typhus and sleeping sickness, than all man's wars put together and we may surmise that the slaughter was proportionately even greater in prehistoric times when human populations were smaller and that much more vulnerable. Agriculturally, too, hordes of locusts, aphids, scale-insects, leafhoppers and caterpillars can cause considerable devastation and even total ruination of crops, not infrequently leading to famine. There are also those other insects which consume stored food products, clothing and upholstery, tunnel into furniture, or even do their best to undermine and destroy the very houses we live in.

The pest status of insects comes about as a direct consequence of one of the main characteristics contributing to their success as a class. It is one that has been stressed elsewhere in this book – their wide-ranging opportunism. If we have something the insects want, be it our blood, food or other materials, then they will come and get it, and it is often extremely difficult to stop them, even with the most powerful pesticides. Apart from the often inadequately investigated side-effects brought about by the use of chemical 'controls', insects tend to be extraordinarily good at developing resistance to their application, a fact which doubtless contributes to the ever-increasing growth of the chemical pest-control industry!

So far as agriculture is concerned, man might even be said to bring trouble from insects upon his own head, since any intensified crop-planting or monoculture is almost certain to attract, in greater numbers, insects preferring that particular plant, with the result that their natural predators are unable to cope. Moreover, exploration and trade has seen to it that insects annoying to man in a variety of ways are spread worldwide, albeit inadvertently. Many plant-sucking bugs, notably Lygaeids and scale-insects, have been presented with an almost cosmopolitan distribution by such means, as have various beetles, ants, springtails and the noxious bed-bug (*Cimex lectularius*). It is said that many of the Pacific Islands were entirely free of fleas until European exploration introduced these annoying parasites, while many commensal insects, such as cockroaches, now exist to scavenge and alarm the nervous in dwellings as far separated as London and Sydney. The true original home of many of these insect travellers is not always clear, but inhabitants of countries where they now flourish are often quick to blame other nations for their infiltration and so, it seems, are scientific naming authorities. The so-called German cockroach (*Blatella germanica*) is dismissed as 'French' by retaliatory Germans but, in fact, is a native of neither country, just as the much larger American cockroach (*Periplaneta americana*) is not indigenous to the USA. Both probably originate from North Africa or the Middle East, but it is difficult to be sure.

Many insect introductions can, of course, only settle and flourish out of doors if the climatic conditions they find in new lands are similar to those in their native countries. This is why some of the most successful are those which take advantage of man's heated dwellings and other buildings. Mention has already been made of cockroaches, but there are other virtually cosmopo-

A common garden pest: larvae of the large white butterfly (*Pieris brassicae*) feeding on a cabbage leaf.

litan species which would probably not manage half as well if they were suddenly rendered homeless, as it were. Species like the pharaoh's ant (*Monomorium pharaonis*), a frequent inhabitant of bakeries, canteens and other well-heated buildings, are tropical in origin and quickly die if their ambient temperature falls to about 5°C (41°F). The notorious museum-beetle (*Anthrenus museorum*), destroyer of many a valuable museum specimen, the bacon-beetle (*Dermestes lardarius*) and the clothes-moth (*Tineola bisselliella*) are all much happier indoors than out and some, such as the fire-brat (*Thermobia domestica*) and the grain-weevil (*Sitophilus granarius*), despoiler of stored grain, are almost never found away from heated premises.

When insects do settle and cause problems out of doors, they may flourish because intensified planting gives them scope and because their natural predators have not arrived with them. It would, in any case, be unrealistic to expect insect and other predators to do more than account for a small proportion of such highly artificial concentrations of plant-feeders, which is precisely why insecticides will probably always be needed as demands for human food become increasingly insistent. Nevertheless, predatory insects (especially parasitic ones) can do an excellent job for man and many of them have been deliberately harnessed as biological controls. Ladybirds, lace-wings, hoverflies, Anthocorid bugs, ichneumon, Chalcid and Braconid wasps have been sent around the world for this purpose, often with highly encouraging results. One of the most spectacularly successful operations of this sort was waged not against an insect but a plant – the prickly pear

Confirmed enemy of the entomologist: larvae of the museum-beetle (*Anthrenus museorum*).

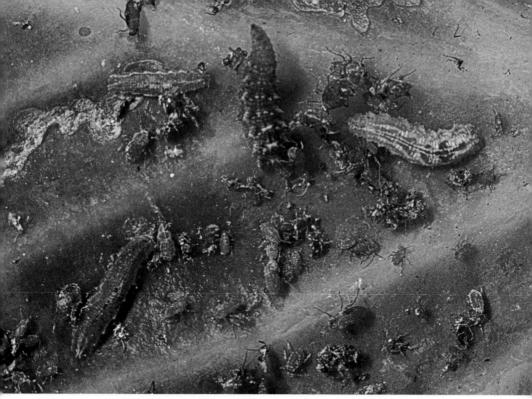

The gardener's friends: larvae of hover-flies (Syrphidae) attacking and eating cabbage aphids. Britain/Europe.

cactus. Apparently originally imported into Australia to form natural livestock fences, the plants had become so rampant by the 1920s that vast areas of grazing land were lost. The problem was solved by the importation from Argentina of supplies of a small moth, *Cactoblastis cactorum*, whose larvae ate into the cactus fronds, causing them to wilt and rot. Millions of hectares of good grazing land were reclaimed as a direct result of the moth's activities. In this case, man was lucky enough to find an insect to get him out of his self-caused difficulty, but redressing the balance is by no means always so easy, as evidenced by the Dutch elm disease which has caused the demise of such a large proportion of elm trees in Britain. Caused by a fungus carried by bark-beetles of the genus *Scolytus*, it seems probable that the most virulent form of the infection was initially spread through the importation of contaminated timber. Such a disease is exceedingly difficult to control, but it is clear that nature and insects are at least doing the best they can to restore the balance since an increase in bark-beetles has been closely followed by something of a population explosion among their predators, notably ant-beetles (*Thanasimus formicarius*) and snake-flies (*Raphidia*).

The value of insects as pollinators is so well known as to require no more than a brief mention, but it is worth emphasising that a great many orchard fruits, vegetables and valuable plants, which produce items such as cocoa, cotton and tobacco, would scarcely flourish at all without visits from nectar- and pollen-seeking insects (by no means all of them bees). Neither, probably, would many of our most admired wild plants, among them orchids, whose flowers are directly designed to attract insect pollinators. Some of these insect-plant relationships are of extraordinary complexity. The tiny New World yucca moth (*Tegeticula yuccasella*), for example, lays her eggs in yucca flowers and in so doing effects cross-pollination, at the same time ensuring the future survival of a quite different group of moths (*Prodoxus*) whose larvae feed only on the plants' stems and seed-pods.

Insects' role as essential scavengers and consumers of noxious waste (see Chapter 6), is scarcely less vital to our interests, but we pay little heed to their useful activities until we find we need them. The introduction of free-range cattle-farming into Australia owes its success, at least partly, to species of African dung-beetles which were imported to consume and break down the cattle dung and return it to the soil. Native Australian scavenging insects, reared on a traditional diet of kangaroo droppings, refused to have anything to do with the aliens' excreta, which thus accumulated and encouraged the growth of weeds unpalatable to the stock. On a less vital, more esoteric level, waste-consuming beetles are still the best at cleaning away the flesh from animals needed for exhibition as museum specimens!

The list of products derived from insects is also a lengthy one. Honey-bees provide us not only with honey but wax for the manufacture of items such as candles, polishes, oils and sealing wax. The manufacture of silk from the so-called silk-worm (*Bombyx mori*) and related species like the tussore silk-moths (*Antheraea*) goes back 4500 years and the demand for it continues, despite the introduction of synthetics. (The silk-worm is now so thoroughly domesti-cated, incidentally, that it cannot survive in the wild.) A scale-insect (*Laccifer lacca*), from India and South-East Asia, provides us with shellac and varnishes, while the Central American bug, *Dactylopius coccus*, yields the cochineal used as a food colouring. Yet another bug, the manna scale-insect (*Trabutina mannipara*), exudes a sugary material after sucking tamarisk trees and this is said to have been the 'manna from heaven' of the Bible. Other scale-insects yield useful products such as waxes.

Insects themselves have long provided man with a source of food, both as a staple part of the diet and in time of crop failure. Huge beetle larvae (especially Cerambycidae), ants, termites, grasshoppers and locusts, and the rather nauseous-looking caterpillars of the goat-moth (*Cossus cossus*) are just some of those insects which appear, or have appeared, on the menu of peoples throughout the world. The nomadic Tuaregs of North Africa make a kind of flour from locusts, while during the 1968 Biafran crisis, the local people fed their children on huge male driver-ants, colloquially referred to as 'sausage-flies'. None of these items would probably be acceptable to Western man and yet the insects are rich in proteins and fats and thus highly nutritious.

Mythology and folklore contain numerous references to insects. The Ancient Egyptians were so fascinated by the determined activities of a dung-beetle (*Scarabaeus sacer*) that they incorporated it and its ball of animal dung in their pantheon – as the symbol of the sun-god, Amon-Ra. Even today, the natives of many tropical areas strongly disapprove of Western collectors of certain crepuscular butterflies, since they consider them to be the souls of their ancestors. Much lore also surrounds such insects as hive-bees, which must be told of any disaster in the family of their human master, as well as dragonflies (commonly called devil's darning-needles and horse-stingers) and crickets and grasshoppers. The appearance of certain ground-beetles is still thought to foretell rain and the belief that earwigs like nothing better than to burrow their way into the ear finds credence right across Europe and elsewhere. In medieval times, the sanctity of mendicant friars tended to be estimated in proportion to the numbers of lice these unwashed gentlemen supported; to be bitten to any great degree was also considered a sure sign of virility.

Medical science has, of course, devoted a considerable amount of time and research into the diseases such parasitic insects as lice and fleas can carry, but many insects have been studied to more positive effect. Cantharidin, synthesised from blister-beetles (Meloidae), has been found to be useful both as a vesicant and for the treatment of certain urinogenital disorders; the curative properties of bee venom are attracting increasing attention, more especially with regard to such conditions as rheumatism and arthritis. Studies of the excretory products of certain blow-flies, such as *Calliphora* and *Lucilia*, have led to the discovery of a substance called *allantoin*, which stimulates the healing of wounds, even when the latter are actually infested by their maggots! When Louis Pasteur was asked, in 1865, to investigate the causes of a baffling disease which was wreaking havoc in the silkworm industry in southern France, he not only solved the problem as one of bacterial infection but was stimulated by his findings to investigate the nature of more serious communicable diseases affecting man. Recent studies of such phenomena as thanatosis, colour change, limb-regeneration and parthenogenesis, especially typical of stick- and leaf-insects, have also produced results of benefit to medical science. Observations of the way insects behave in conditions of overcrowding, e.g. locusts preparing for migration, may afford valuable clues as to why human neurological stress and crime is greater in towns than elsewhere.

The seemingly insignificant fruit-fly (*Drosophila*) has proved of considerable value in studying the mechanism of heredity, since not only does it breed easily and prolifically in captivity but has unusually large and readily discernible *chromosomes*, the structures directly concerned with the transfer of genetic material to its descendants. Equally fascinating is the insight afforded by a comparison of those parasites afflicting different hosts, perhaps suggesting evolutionary relationships. It is surely not without significance that the pubic louse living on gorillas is of a species very closely related to that which occasionally afflicts man!

Despite his suspicion of much of the tribe, man has long recognised the matchless beauty of many insects and the more esoteric appeal of others. The

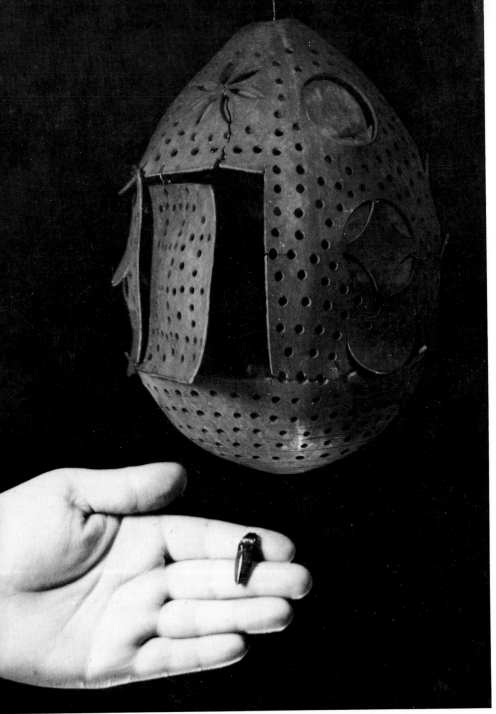

A firefly lantern from Dominica, Leeward Islands, made from a gourd. A specimen of the Neotropical firefly, *Pyrophorus noctilucus*, several of which were used to provide the illumination, is held in the hand to indicate its size.

brilliant colours of butterflies like the 'blues', Morphos and birdwings, as well as many beetles, has long made them the object of collectors, artistic seekers of inspiration and decorators of living rooms. In Ancient Greece, and more recently in China and Japan, crickets were kept in cages for the better appreciation of their songs or, less happily, reared to fight. Even today, the Japanese imprison fireflies in special lanterns or hold open-air firefly-viewing festivals for the aesthetic pleasure afforded by their delightful greenish glow and, at one time, poor Eastern students actually used them to read by. Natives of Brazil and the West Indies once used the powerfully luminescent *Pyrophorus* firefly to illuminate their huts or for nocturnal hunting expeditions.

To the casual observer, it often seems that it is just the more directly appealing insects of this kind that suffer a decline, whereas pest species thrive despite all our efforts to reduce them. Collecting, *per se*, is only rarely to blame; indeed the activities of collectors have added, and can add, greatly to our knowledge of insects, provided that their material is fully documented. More often, the cause lies deeper, in habitat destruction or interference. In Britain, for example, the delightful field cricket (*Gryllus campestris*) and mole-cricket (*Gryllotalpa gryllotalpa*) are both now considerable rarities and the glow-worm beetle (*Lampyris noctiluca*) is an infinitely less familiar sight than it was about 30–40 years ago. Such species tend to have rather specialised habitat requirements and also, to some extent, are at the northernmost limit of their natural range, so that they do not react favourably to the changes in

Cricket and cicada cages from China, Japan and Malaya. All specimens are from the Horniman Museum, London.

land-use which have effected their decline. The same can be said, to an even greater degree, of the large blue butterfly (*Maculinea arion*), which depends for its survival on a whole range of interdependent circumstances, including the presence of *Myrmica* ants and a well-cropped terrain, but has now apparently been finally extinguished in Britain as a result of man-induced environmental changes.

Despite the adaptability of the class as a whole, insects like these are constantly walking a tightrope between survival and extinction, as, too, for slightly different reasons, are hosts of brilliant or bizarre, large or small species that exist in the world's fast-disappearing tropical forests and nowhere else. Sadly, while laws are passed to protect and prevent the collection of individual species, both in Europe and the USA and in the jungles of New Guinea and South America, much less is being done to conserve the habitats they live in. Environmental conservation is indeed the key, for we are talking here not only of insects but of whole ecosystems, of which the insects are a vital, fascinating and wholly delightful part.

Chapter 16
Nomenclature and Classification

The use of popular or colloquial names for insects, however attractive and revealing they may be, can cause considerable confusion. Even within the English language the same or very similar names are quite often used for quite different insects. Thus 'black-fly' can refer to both biting Diptera of the family Simulidae and sucking bugs (*Aphis fabae*) that attack broad beans; in Britain, 'glow-worms' are sexually dimorphic beetles (*Lampyris noctiluca*), whereas, in New Zealand, they are the luminous larvae of a species of fly (*Arachnocampa luminosa*). The names themselves can give a misleading idea of the nature and kinship of the insects concerned, e.g. 'water-crickets' and 'water-stick-insects' are Heteropterid bugs and quite unrelated to the Orthoptera and Phasmida. This is to say nothing of the problems of identification arising through correspondence between entomologists in different countries if only the native language is used to describe the subjects under discussion.

An international system of terminology is thus essential for the study of insects, just as it is in every other branch of natural history. Essentially such a naming system is based on Latin, Latinised Greek, or what might be called 'dog Latin'. The basic unit of classification is the *species*: essentially an interbreeding group which is genetically distinct and unable to breed with other similar groups. When crosses (*hybrids*) do occur between species, the progeny are usually sterile and unable to breed; an ability to hybridise is also an indication of the species' close relationship.

Normally a species is given two names which are always used in conjunction and never separately: the generic name (always with an initial capital) comes first followed by a specific name (in lower case). In purely scientific writing, the species' name is then followed by the name of the person who first described the insect, generally abbreviated. Thus, *Pieris brassicae* L. (or Linn.) is the full name of the large or cabbage white butterfly, the last abbreviation indicating that it was named by Carl von Linné (Linnaeus), the great eighteenth-century Swedish naturalist, who devised the *binomial system* of classification of animals and plants that we know today. Sometimes a third name is added after the specific one to indicate a geographical race, form or subspecies, which differs in minor ways from the typical species. For example, *Papilio machaon britannicus* is the purely British race of the swallowtail butterfly whose wider distribution extends right across Europe as far east as Japan.

A genus of insects usually comprises a number of different species and the generic name is the same for each, clearly indicating their close relationship. Thus, we have a number of species of 'white' butterfly, all belonging to the genus *Pieris*. (*Pieris* is commonly abbreviated to '*P.*' when they are being mentioned or described together, e.g. *Pieris brassicae*, *P. rapae*, *P. napi*). Genera, in turn, are grouped into families or in some cases subfamilies (whose names end in '-idae' and '-inae' respectively); families may also be incorporated into superfamilies (ending in '-oidea'), and the latter into suborders, until, finally, we have the 29 full orders comprising the class Insecta. The whole system is designed not just to name the insects but to indicate the degree of relationship between them.

The insect orders themselves are subject to further grouping. The first four are collectively called Apterygota (wingless insects) and are the most primitive of the Insecta, so much so that many authorities do not consider them to be proper insects at all. The other twenty-five orders comprise the Pterygota (winged insects) but are subdivided into Exopterygote (or Hemimetabolous) insects (p. 184) and Endopterygote (or Holometabolous) insects (p. 198).

The classification given follows that outlined in the tenth edition of *Imms' General Textbook of Entomology* (Richards & Davies, 1977), a classic work that no entomologist can afford to be without. It should be pointed out that the numbers of species given are often extremely approximate and, in many cases, are constantly being added to, as new species are discovered and named.

Insect Orders

Apterygota

Telson-tails – Protura (Greek *protos* first or simple; *oura* tail) *c.* 200 species. Worldwide. Fig. 16.1

Only familiar to zoology since 1907, the Protura are among the least known of all the insects, principally because of their minute size (up to *c.* 2 mm or $\frac{1}{125}$ in) and secretive habits. Living mostly in the soil, they lack wings and are also eyeless and virtually colourless. Unique among insects in lacking antennae, the sensory role of which seems primarily assumed by the forwardly directed forelegs, proturans also grow in a distinctive manner. On hatching from the egg, the proturan has eight abdominal segments, but at each subsequent ecdysis adds another, bringing the total to eleven. No other insects grow in quite this way and none has more than ten abdominal segments. At the end of the abdomen is a structure called a telson, which is absent in all other adult insects, although it is characteristic of other

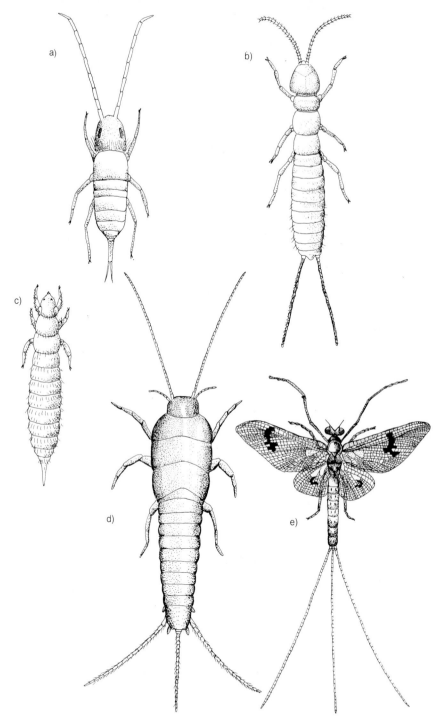

Fig. 16.1. a) Springtail (Collembola). b) Two-pronged bristletail (Diplura). c) Proturan. d) Three-pronged bristletail (Thysanura). e) Mayfly (Ephemeroptera).

arthropods, notably crustaceans. Another feature linking proturans with crustaceans is the jointed, limb-like stylets on each of the first three abdominal segments, comparable with those possessed by crabs, lobsters and crayfish. Proturans are probably principally waste-feeders, although some are known to consume fungi, and may also use the sharp claws at the tips of the forelegs for impaling other minute animals, whose contents are then sucked out by the piercing mouthparts. Some proturans have also been observed to curve the telson over the head and discharge a sticky secretion at their enemies; otherwise this terminal appendage seems mainly used in locomotion.

Springtails – Collembola (Greek *kolla* to fasten together; *embolon* a peg or wedge) *c.* 2000 species. Worldwide. Fig. 16.1

The popular name of this primitive group of insects refers to their highly idiosyncratic method of leaping, involving a forked device which is doubled up under the body when at rest. Perhaps the most numerous in populations of all the insects, springtails are found in the soil, beneath leaf litter and heaps of decaying vegetation and also in old birds' nests. They feed principally on decomposing plant material and occur in such numbers that they must be considered among the most important of all insects for breaking down and returning such matter to the soil, thus enriching it. Rarely longer than about 5 mm ($\frac{1}{5}$ in), most springtails are drably coloured with antennae varying in length, although consisting of only four to six segments. Some species are elongated in shape, others are stubby and more rounded, e.g. the greenish *Sminthurus viridis* which, untypically, consumes living plant material and has proved something of a pest in parts of Africa and Australia.

Structurally the group is unique among insects in having an abdomen of only six segments and simple undifferentiated tarsal leg joints, like those of larval insects. On the underside of the springtail's abdomen is a ventral tube which is variously considered to be concerned with respiration, water absorption or to act as an adhesive organ enabling locomotion over slippery surfaces. In general, springtails prefer damp conditions and some are semi-aquatic. *Podura aquatica* lives on the surface of ponds, while others, such as the bluish grey *Anurida maritima*, gather in close-packed clusters on coastal pools, the last-mentioned species lacking a springing device, despite being periodically immersed by the tides. The group's tolerance of varied conditions, is, however, indicated by the fact that some species live in deserts and caves, while species of *Isotoma* ('snow-flea') are alpine and often active on snow and ice in very low temperatures; others exist as scavengers in the nests of ants and termites. The Collembola are the oldest known of all the insects, having come down to the present virtually unchanged from the Devonian period, some 400 million years ago.

Two-pronged Bristletails – Diplura (Greek *diplos* double; *oura* tail) *c.* 600 species. Worldwide. Fig. 16.1

Typical soil-dwellers, diplurans are not surprisingly often both colourless and blind, since neither pigment nor vision is needed in what is, at most, a twilight world. Most species are no more than a few millimetres long. One of the best known families of the order is the near cosmopolitan Campodeidae, typified by the all-white *Campodea staphylinus*, which occurs under stones, old logs and occasionally in garden ants' nests, where it probably acts as a scavenger. Only 3–5 mm $(\frac{1}{10} - \frac{1}{5}$ in$)$ long, it nevertheless includes in this length long 'beaded' antennae and also a pair of even longer tail appendages (cerci) which provide the order with its common and scientific names. A second family, the Japygidae, differ in having their cerci in the form of a hardened, pincer-like fork, with which they seize small soil-dwelling arthropods (such as springtails) as food. Japygids have a more restricted distribution than the Campodeidae, occurring in southern Europe, North America and Australia. Some Australian species of *Japyx* attain a length of 50 mm (2 in). A third family, the Projapygidae, are few in species and restricted to tropical and subtropical areas. To varying degrees, diplurans are prone to desiccation and extremely light-shy, making them difficult to study. Consequently, much less is known of their habits and life history than of other orders (this applies to all the Apterygota). One interesting feature that has been observed in some diplurans, however, is a kind of primitive maternal care for the young nymphs, which hatch from eggs laid and protected within a small earthen chamber.

Three-pronged Bristletails – Thysanura (Greek *thusanos* fringe; *oura* tail) *c.* 550 species. Worldwide. Fig. 16.1

Thysanurans are characterised by their long antennae, three tail filaments and tapering body, which is covered in tiny overlapping scales, easily removed on the finger, although some species and early stages have reduced scaling. The most widely familiar species is the silverfish (*Lepisma saccharina*), frequently found in damp houses, bathrooms and kitchens, where it scavenges on starchy and sugar substances, including book bindings and wallpaper paste. Another is the so-called firebrat (*Thermobia domestica*), which is adapted to living at high temperatures and is thus, outside of warmer climates, most commonly found in bakeries and similar heated premises. Some moderately large (*c.* 10 mm or $\frac{2}{5}$ in) species of *Dilta* have an attractive lustrous metallic sheen and live in leaf litter, more especially in woodlands, while others (e.g. *Petrobius*) occur among rocks around the coasts. A number of minute species, like *Atelura*, live as scavengers or semi-predators in the nests of ants and termites, while others are cave-dwellers. Thysanurans are typically fast-movers and light-shy; silverfish for example will run in a rapid sinuous fashion over walls and make for cover when exposed to light. As silverfish have only small compound eyes and no ocelli (although outdoor species display a greater development of both), it seems that the whole body must be sensitive to light. Being virtually omnivorous, the bristletails' mouthparts are primarily adapted for biting and chewing.

The name Thysanura refers to the fringes of hairs that decorate the sides of the tail filaments.

Pterygota

EXOPTERYGOTA These insects undergo an incomplete metamorphosis with no proper pupal stage, hence their alternative name, Hemimetabola.

Mayflies – Ephemeroptera (Greek *ephemeros* living for a day; *pteron* wing) *c.* 2000 species. Worldwide. Fig. 16.1

Adult mayflies are fragile creatures with delicate tissue-like wings, often displaying a pearly lustre. The hind pair are much the smaller and, in some groups, e.g. *Cleon*, are absent altogether. In all cases, flight is weak and the wings can only be held together in a vertical position when the insect is at rest. The legs are often strongly developed, the forepair being, in the male, commonly much longer than the others as they are used for gripping the female during mating; they are, however, virtually useless for walking, many species of mayflies being almost helpless when on the ground. Most species have two or three very long tail filaments which may act as balancers during flight but are easily lost. The antennae are very short and inconspicuous but the compound eyes are well developed, larger in the male, and in some groups divided into two sections – the upper pair having larger ommatidia. Adult mayflies are unable to feed, having degenerate mouthparts and no proper digestive tract. They are often extremely shortlived, whereas the aquatic larvae may spend several years in lake, pond or river before leaving the water and transforming into adults. Mayfly nymphs vary in shape, some being flattened to counteract strong currents as they cling to the river bed, others being more tubular and adapted for burrowing. They feed mostly on minute planktonic plants and animals and are unique among Pterygote larvae in possessing mouthparts of the crustacean type, an indication of the group's primitiveness. Mayflies are also the only insects to exhibit a pre-adult winged form, the *sub-imago* or 'dun', which undergoes a further moult before being able to fly and mate.

Dragonflies and Damselflies – Odonata (Greek *odos* a tooth) *c.* 5000 species. Worldwide. Fig. 16.2

The Odonata are sub-divided into two sub-orders: the Anisoptera, embracing the larger 'hawker' and 'darter' dragonflies, and the Zygoptera or damselflies. The former are the more powerfully built insects, with large compound eyes which occupy a greater part of the head and wings that can be held only laterally when at rest; the hindwings are somewhat smaller than the forewings (Greek *anis* unequal). Damselflies are more delicately built, with a much less powerful, more fluttering flight; the wings are more equal in size and typically folded together (Greek *zygon* yoke) when the insects settle

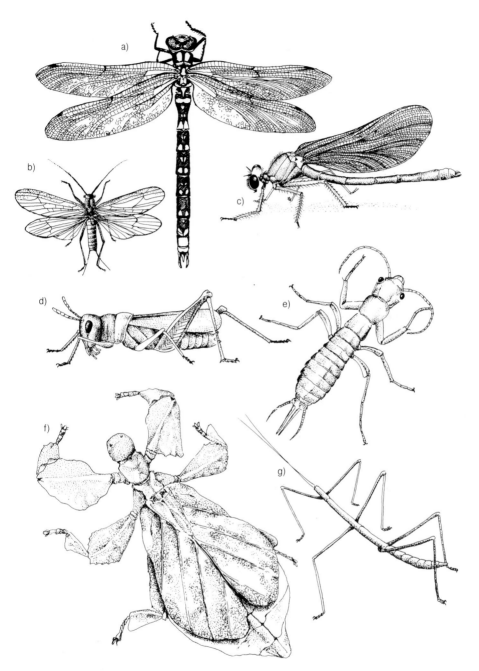

Fig. 16.2. a) Dragonfly (Odonata: Anisoptera). b) Stone-fly (Plecoptera). c) Damsel-fly (Odonata: Zygoptera). d) Grasshopper (Orthoptera). e) Cricket-cockroach (Grylloblattodea). f) Leaf-insect (Phasmida). g) Stick-insect (Phasmida).

on vegetation, although they can also be extended laterally; their eyes are large but more widely separated on the head than in Anisoptera, giving a dumb-bell appearance. Both groups have very short antennae but this is compensated for by their exceedingly keen vision. Many dragonflies are powerful, restless fliers, especially 'hawkers', and species of *Anax* have been recorded as attaining speeds of about 30 km/hr (18 mph) while *Austrophlebia* is thought to be able to fly at over three times that rate. Several species, such as the European *Libellula quadrimaculata* (a darter dragonfly), are well known migrators. The Odonata are often brilliantly coloured, perhaps with bright scarlet head and body, and with a red flush on the wings, as in species of European *Sympetrum* and the African *Brachythemis*. The male *Libellula depressa* has the abdomen coloured a delightful Cambridge blue, in contrast to the male *Agrion virgo* damselfly, whose body and wings are a uniform deepest metallic blue. Such colouration is typical of male Odonata, females being generally duller. While most of the larger and more powerful members of the order belong to the Anisoptera, the largest member of the Odonata known today is a damselfly, the South American *Megaloprepus coerulatus*, with a wing span of some 190 mm ($7\frac{1}{2}$ in). Extinct dragonflies attained a very much greater size. Wing impressions of *Meganeura monyi* found at Commentry, France, indicate that it had a wingspan in excess of 700 mm (28 in) and is the largest insect known to have inhabited the earth. Together with mayflies, the Odonata are among the oldest and most primitive of the insects, dating back at least to the Upper Carboniferous, some 300 million years ago. Only recently a new fossil species of this age was discovered in a Derbyshire coalmine; it had a wing span of 500 mm (nearly 20 in) and has been named *Typhus diluculum*. Dragonfly and damselfly nymphs are almost invariably fully aquatic, breathing by means of internal gills in the Anisoptera and by three external lamellae in the Zygoptera. Like the adults, which capture their prey on the wing, they are wholly predacious, capturing their prey with a unique, extensible mask equipped with fangs at the tip. The nymphs are often long-lived, spending anything from 2–4 years in this stage; adults generally live for about a year.

Stoneflies – Plecoptera (Greek *plekein* fold; *pteron* wing) *c.* 3000 species. Worldwide. Fig. 16.2

Stoneflies are another ancient group of insects whose early stages, like those of mayflies and dragonflies, are spent in water. Their scientific name refers to the characteristic folding of the adults' delicate, transparent wings when at rest, one overlapping the other, often so as to almost completely cover and enclose the abdomen. In the thin-bodied Leuctridae, the appearance is that of a tightly rolled umbrella. The underwings are, in most species, much wider than the forepair. The adult stonefly typically has long antennae, a pair of conspicuous tail filaments and, in larger species, a comparatively heavy tubular body, with a head of about the same width.

Most are sluggish and reluctant fliers and are usually seen clinging to stones or vegetation or crawling over the ground near lakes and rivers. They are generally dully coloured, usually some shade of dark brown, green or yellow. Having poorly developed mouthparts, the adults often do not feed at all during their short life, although their flattened nymphs may be either predatory or herbivorous. The nymphs are often extremely tolerant of cold and even some adults mate in winter in the northern hemisphere. Nearly all species are extremely intolerant of pollution so that their presence or absence is an indication of the health of rivers or streams.

'Cricket-Cockroaches' – Grylloblattodea (Latin *gryllus* cricket; *blatta* cockroach) 16 known species. Probably Nearctic only. Fig. 16.2

These curious 'halfway' insects were only made known to science in 1914, when the first species (*Grylloblatta campodeiformis*) was discovered in the Canadian Rockies. They are considered sufficiently distinct to justify separate ordinal status since they exhibit features which seem to place them somewhere between crickets and cockroaches, e.g. their large cockroach-like coxae and the female's ovipositor, which is closer in structure to that of the Orthoptera. Since the first species was discovered, a number of others have come to light in the USSR, the USA and Canada, and it is now thought that Grylloblattids may be the 'living fossil' descendants of a group which gave rise to today's Orthoptera, Dictyoptera, Mantodea and Phasmida. Averaging about 2.5 cm (1 in) in length, wingless and with reduced or absent eyes, Grylloblattids generally live beneath moss and stones, often at high altitude, where they seem able to tolerate very low temperatures.

Grasshoppers, Groundhoppers, Bush-Crickets, Crickets, etc. – Orthoptera (Greek *orthos* straight; *pteron* wing) or **Saltatoria** (Latin *saltare* to jump) Over 17 000 species. Worldwide. Fig. 16.2

The alternative name of this large and diverse order draws immediate attention to one of its members' most obvious characters – the ability to jump. However, some Orthoptera are only feeble leapers and others appear to have discarded such athleticism altogether. Sound-production by means of stridulation is another feature of the group and is principally employed by males as a courtship signal, although in some species the female emits an answering call. A number of species do not stridulate but communicate by pattering the substrate with their feet or abdomen or by grinding together their mandibular plates; others use wing signals or various glandular secretions. Precise details of Orthopteran classification are the subject of some difference of opinion but two main suborders are recognised. The Caelifera includes the grasshoppers, locusts and groundhoppers or 'bush locusts', characterised mainly by very short antennae, long hind legs (with broad femora) and long wings, which open out like a fan and are protected and covered by leathery forewings or tegmina; stridulation in caeliferans is effected by rubbing a raised ridge on the enlarged femur against a hardened edge of the tegmen. The Ensifera, the other suborder, comprises the bush-crickets, true crickets, mole-crickets and some other families, all of which are characterised by sometimes exceedingly long thread-like antennae; occasionally members of the group lack operative wings, although the tegmina remain for stridulation purposes, sound production being effected by rubbing one tegmen over the other. Another distinction between the two suborders lies in the female ensiferans' possession of a large ovipositor, which is commonly curved and sabre-like in bush-crickets and straight and tapering in true crickets. Grasshoppers and their allies display no external ovipositor. Unlike their relatives, grasshoppers are diurnal in habit, most species being cryptically camouflaged to match vegetation, although the underwings in some groups (such as *Oedipoda*) are brilliantly coloured – red or blue. Locusts are no more than large grasshoppers, differing principally in their tendency to periodically migrate in large numbers. Groundhoppers, by contrast, are among the smallest of the Caelifera and are always solitary in their habits; short and stumpy in appearance, they display a characteristic extension of the thorax called the *pronotum* which covers almost the entire length of the abdomen. Bush-crickets are commonly called long-horned grasshoppers or katydids, but both names are misleading since they are more closely related to the true crickets (Gryllidae), while 'katydid' is an onomatopoeic name referring principally to American species. Some tropical bush-crickets are among the largest of all insects, e.g. *Siliquofera grandis* from New Guinea has a wing span of over 250 mm (10 in). Related to the bush-crickets are the curious, wingless camel-crickets, some of which are found only in caves as Ice Age relics, while others, such as the greenhouse camel-cricket (*Tachycines asynamorus*), have become established in colder countries as residents in heated greenhouses. Another family (Stenopelmatidae) includes the enormous king-crickets and wetas of Africa and Australasia, the males of which have huge mandibles and a somewhat ferocious appearance. True crickets are commonly wingless and include the cosmopolitan house-cricket (*Acheta domesticus*), Dickens' 'cricket on the hearth', the sturdy shiny black field-cricket (*Gryllus campestris*) and many other species, some of which live in arid or desert areas, such as the curiously colourless *Comicus* of the African Namib desert. Most of the Gryllidae are ground-dwellers, although the tree-crickets (*Oecanthus*) construct their nests of rolled leaves joined with silk in trees and bushes. Mole-crickets (*Gryllotalpa*), characterised by their rather musical continuous reeling call, are of particular interest since they seem to exhibit evolutionary adaptations parallel to those of moles, notably in the shape and position of their forelegs, which are strengthened for soil excavation; they can fly quite well, having large membranous wings which support the heavy, pendulous abdomen.

Stick-Insects, and Leaf-Insects – Phasmida (Greek *phasma* an apparition) *c.* 2500 species. Widespread; mainly tropical. Fig. 16.2

Allied to the Orthoptera and Dictyoptera (cockroaches), stick- and leaf-insects are especially typical of tropical regions, probably the greatest number of species being found in South-East Asia. Most have thread-like antennae of variable length, with rather small eyes. Of the two groups, stick-insects are especially characterised by the considerable elongation of the mesothorax, resulting in wide separation of the legs; this, together with their typical green or brown colouration, heightens their cryptic twig-like appearance. Some species have their legs and body decorated with thorn-like spines. When disturbed, the insects may also draw up their legs close to and parallel with the body and feign death. While many stick-insects are flightless, others have wings which are large and brightly coloured; sometimes the protective forewings (tegmina) are absent, in which case the leading, anterior edge of the operative wings is toughened to assume a protective role – the whole opening out like a fan when in use. Some species of stick-insect occur in southern Europe, but the well-known laboratory stick-insect (*Carausius morosus*) is probably Asiatic in origin. Leaf-insects (*Phyllium* etc.) occur mainly in the Australo-Oriental region and differ from stick-insects in having their forewings (useless for flight) elaborated into an extraordinarily leaf-like shape, complete with veins; the legs may also bear leaf-like expansions. All Phasmids are predominantly vegetarian and live mostly in dense shrubbery, where they remain immobile during much of the day. Many species possess the ability to change colour according to light intensity, temperature and humidity, becoming darker at night and paler during the day. An interesting feature of the group is that in some species males are either rare or entirely absent and, as a result, reproduction is parthenogenetic. Stick-insects include the longest (if not the bulkiest) of all the insects. The tropical *Pharnacia serratipes* attains a length of some 330 mm (13 in), while others, such as *Palophus titan* and *Phoboeticus fruhstorferi*, are almost as large.

Earwigs – Dermaptera (Greek *derma* skin; *pteron* wing) *c.* 1200 species. Worldwide. Fig. 16.3

A characteristic feature of the Dermaptera is the large sclerotised pincers at the end of the abdomen, which are usually strongly curved and caliper-like in the male but smaller and straighter in the female; in both sexes, they seem to be used primarily for defence and are spread and curved over the body if the insects are threatened. Typically, earwigs have large, exceedingly delicate tissue-like wings, although this is not immediately obvious since they are multi-folded beneath short, waistcoat-like tegmina, not unlike the elytra of rove-beetles (see Coleoptera); moreover species like the common earwig (*Forficula auricularia*) do not fly with any great readiness, suggesting an increasing adaptation to entirely terrestrial living. Others, such as the 8–10 mm ($\frac{1}{10} - \frac{4}{10}$ in) long *Labia minor*, fly readily, but are infrequently seen. The cosmopolitan *Forficula auricularia*, on the other hand, is probably one of the most familiar of all insects, having extended its range from Europe to almost every other continent. Particularly common in gardens and under bark, the common earwig is predominantly omnivorous or waste-feeding, a habit which has been taken to more specialised lengths in certain Indonesian species which feed on bat droppings in caves. Other species are ectoparasites on the bats themselves (*Arixenia*) or on various kinds of rats in Africa (*Hemimerus*). The bat-parasite, *Arixenia esau*, is the largest of all mammalian ectoparasites, while other free-living earwig species are considerably larger. The giant earwig (*Labidura herculeana*) of St Helena attains a length of 80 mm (3 in) and there are also some unusually large species in Australia (e.g. *Titanolabis collossea* and *Apachypus australiae*). A number of Dermaptera live on the seashore and others, such as *Prolabia arachidis*, have become adapted to living in heated premises such as greenhouses. A feature of many earwig species is the devotion they show to their eggs and nymphs. At one time the group was classified with the Orthoptera, with whom they share a number of structural affinities.

Web-spinners – Embioptera (Greek *embios* living; *pteron* wing). Over 300 species. Widespread. Fig. 16.3

Web-spinners are little-known insects, rather like earwigs or termites in appearance, except that the tail cerci are soft and jointed and the wings (when present) are darker than those of termites, although much the same size. In fact, female web-spinners are invariably wingless and males often so, especially in European species. The group gains its popular name from the silk-lined tunnels and webs which the insects construct beneath stones and in the soil; the silk is produced by special glands on the basal segment of the fore-tarsi (no other insects produce silk by this means). The silken cover acts both as a protection against predators and as a means of maintaining a micro-climate. Web-spinners tend to live communally, the females commonly guarding their eggs and nymphs, thus indicating the rudiments of social organisation. Mostly rather small (c.4–8 mm or $\frac{1}{10} - \frac{3}{10}$ in), web-spinners are represented in most of the world's natural regions but are commoner in the tropics and sub-tropics.

Cockroaches and Mantids – Dictyoptera (Greek *dictyon* net; *pteron* wing) c. 6000 species. Widespread. Fig. 16.3

At first sight, it appears somewhat perverse that two such apparently distinct groups of insects should be placed in the same order and, indeed, some entomologists still prefer to give cockroaches (suborder Blattaria) and mantids (Mantodea) separate ordinal status. However, the two display many structural similarities, notably in the *hypognathous* (downwardly directed) triangular head armed with biting mouthparts, the fan-like wings, covered and protected by toughened forewings or tegmina, and in the manner of depositing their eggs in oothecae (a feature also shared by grasshoppers). Cockroaches are superficially not unlike certain beetles in general appearance, but, like mantids, bear a pair of stubby cerci at the tail, a feature never displayed by the Coleoptera. Mainly omnivorous or waste-

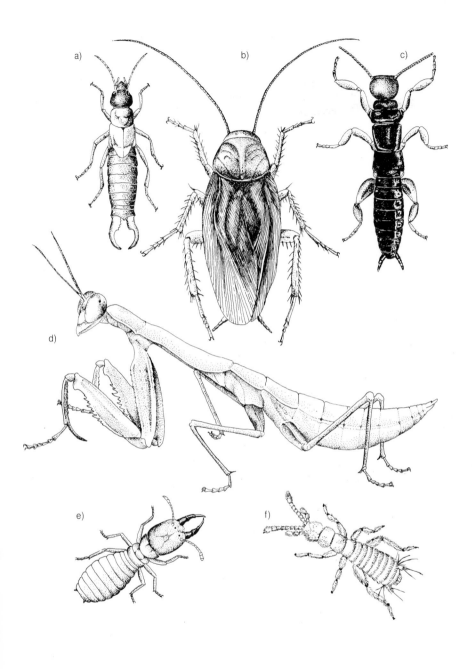

Fig. 16.3. a) Earwig (Dermaptera). b) Cockroach (Dictyoptera). c) Web-spinner (Embioptera). d) Mantid (Dictyoptera). e) Termite (Isoptera). f) Zorapteran.

feeders, some species of cockroaches have become established as commensals of man, e.g. *Blatta orientalis* (common cockroach), polished black in colour, and the so-called American and German cockroaches, all of which are probably Asiatic or African in origin. The Australian *Periplaneta australasiae* is another species extending its range in this manner. Many other species live out of doors, especially in the tropics, and some of them are very large, e.g. the South American *Monostria similis* and the cryptically coloured *Eublaberus*. The African Cape mountain cockroach (*Aptera congulata*) is another very large species (40 mm or $1\frac{1}{2}$ in). Cockroaches have a characteristic extension of the thorax (pronotum) which covers most of the head, a feature absent in mantids. Both (especially cockroaches) have long antennae and the eyes are especially large and visually acute in mantids. Typically, cockroaches are nocturnal, their long legs enabling them to scuttle rapidly out of the light; by contrast, mantids are diurnal and slow movers, using their specially adapted forelegs, armed with spines, for seizing and holding prey. When threatened or stalking prey, the mantid raises its forelegs in an anticipatory manner which has prompted the epithet 'praying'. (The word *mantis* is Greek for 'prophet' or 'seer'.) Many mantids are superbly camouflaged to resemble leaves or flowers, a feature which, coupled with slow, deliberate movements, enables them to get close to their intended victims or, in turn, to avoid detection by their own enemies, such as birds and lizards. Some present an appearance which would seem to render them perfect models for the science-fiction film-maker's idea of an invader from outer space. The South American *Stenophylla cornigera*, for example, bears curious horn-like extensions on the head which, together with the large, widely separated eyes, triangular head and rapacious jaws, give the insect a fearsome, devilish appearance when viewed head-on. A characteristic behavioural feature of mantids lies in the females' summary treatment of males, which are commonly attacked and eaten, even during the mating process. Mantids and cockroaches may be either winged or wingless, and some tropical species are frequently attracted to artificial light, although flight is not a characteristic of the order as a whole.

Termites – Isoptera (Greek *isos* equal, similar; *pteron* wing) *c.* 1900 species. Tropics, sub-tropics and warm temperate areas. Fig. 16.3

Apart from the Hymenoptera, termites (often misleadingly called 'white ants') are the only insects to have developed a fully social life. One essential difference between the two is that termite nymphs are fully active from the start, unlike the helpless larvae of Hymenoptera, and often take a part in running the community. Moreover, termite workers may be both male and female and, in their early stages at least, are capable of becoming full sexuals, whereas workers of ants, bees and wasps are always sterile females. In termite communities, also, the adult males, or kings, play a continuous part and mate with the queen at regular intervals, whereas male Hymenoptera usually die quickly after mating.

Typically, termites are soft-bodied insects, whitish or colourless, with strong biting mouthparts for chewing e.g. leaves, seeds, wood. As their scientific name suggests, their two pairs of wings (only present in sexual castes) are of similar size; they are also delicate and incapable of sustaining prolonged flight. Even within a single community, there is often very considerable difference in caste size. Soldiers, for example, may have greatly enlarged chitinised heads and massive mandibles for defence (e.g. Kalotermitidae) or bear a curious snout-like extension on the head with which they are able to spray intruders with an incapacitating gummy secretion (Termitidae and Rhinotermitidae). Males are generally larger than the ordinary workers, with unspecialised heads and mouthparts, and queens sometimes attain a very considerable size, with grossly enlarged, egg-filled abdomens, more especially in the Termitidae, whose queens are sometimes quite enormous.

Termites' nests vary considerably, from primitive structures in decaying wood to vast *termitaria*, like man-made dolmens in appearance, which are especially typical of African *Macrotermes* and the Australian *Nasutitermes*. Dry-wood termites (Kalotermitidae), which abound in the tropics as well as southern Europe, can sometimes cause considerable damage by boring tunnels into structural timbers. Some wood-eating termites, such as the Australian *Masotermes darwiniensis*, display features indicating a close relationship to cockroaches, notably in laying their eggs in purse-like capsules by means of an ovipositor of the cockroach-type, the lack of functional wings (common in cockroaches) and the possession of similar symbiotic micro-organisms in the gut for breaking down cellulose.

One interesting feature termites share with Hymenoptera (especially ants), is the variety of tiny animals commonly existing in their nests as uninvited guests, either as scavengers or minor predators, ranging from springtails, bristletails, bugs, moth and fly larvae, to centipedes and millipedes. Sometimes, too, colonies of ants and termites may share the same earth system, the relationship being usually an amicable one unless the ants are disturbed. Termite nest populations range from a few dozen in more primitive groups to hundreds of thousands in the large mound-builders.

Zorapterans – Zoraptera (Greek *zoros* completely; Latin *a* without; Greek *pteron*, wing) Widespread, not Palaearctic. 22 known species. Fig. 16.3

Zorapterans are minute (up to 3 mm or $\frac{1}{10}$ in) insects which few people, even entomologists, have ever seen. They were only made known to science in 1913 when the first (wingless) specimen was described in an Italian entomological journal. Since then, winged forms have been discovered and it is now known that both winged and wingless forms may occur within the same species. Some species appear to lose their wings after mating, fracturing them roughly at the base rather as do termites, to which the Zoraptera are considered to be closely related. Apparently confined to warm, humid climates (notably the Americas and South-East Asia), the insects live in semi-social groups in decaying wood, under bark or in the ground, sometimes in association with termites, feeding on fungi as well as tiny animals, such as mites. Like termites and cockroaches, they are extremely light-shy, with long legs for rapid running and conspicuously beaded antennae.

Book-Lice, etc. – Psocoptera (Greek *psocus* to grind; *pteron* wing) *c.* 2000 species. Worldwide. Fig. 16.4

In some respects 'lice' is a misleading term for these minute insects since they are not parasitic and do not suck blood, but are mainly scavengers. Ranging in size from about 1–7 mm ($\frac{1}{25} - \frac{1}{4}$ in), often with rather round abdomens, many species occur indoors where they live beneath peeling wallpaper, in upholstery or in the bindings of old books from which they may commonly be shaken. Such species are almost invariably wingless, pale or colourless, but outdoor Psocids, living on vegetation or on or under bark, may be fully winged and coloured varying shades of green, brown or black, some species being distinctively striped or with tiny metallic scales and looking like minute spiders. Occasionally there are fully winged and short-winged or entirely apterous individuals within the same species, the latter frequenting lower parts of vegetation with those able to fly living at a higher level. Some bark-living species tend to be gregarious, even moving about in the same direction like sheep. Indoor-living Psocids have poorly developed eyes and some of them (e.g. *Liposcelis divinatorius*) apparently communicate by means of sound, tapping a substrate with a callosity at the end of the abdomen and producing a faint but distinct ticking. Such species are colloquially called 'ticking spiders' and, like the death-watch beetle, were once widely thought to presage a death in the family with their mysterious tappings. An interesting feature of the group is that both adults and larvae are able to spin silk from the labium, this being used as a protective web for adults, eggs and larvae.

Biting-Lice, Bird-Lice – Mallophaga (Greek *mallos* wool; *phagein* to eat) *c.* 2800 species. Worldwide. Fig. 16.4

The Mallophaga are another group of very minute insects that live as ectoparasites of birds and occasionally mammals. Their mouthparts are adapted for chewing rather than piercing so they feed mainly on skin fragments, dermal secretions, feathers and hair, although a few feed on their host's blood, especially from wounds. They differ principally from members of the succeeding order, with which they are sometimes combined as the Phthiraptera (Greek *phtheir* louse; *aptera* wingless), both in their feeding habits and usually in the greater size and width of the head. They have long oval bodies, short antennae and clawed feet for clinging to their host's feathers etc. Lacking wings or an ability to jump, mallophagans sometimes hitch a ride to alternative hosts on blood-sucking flies and fleas – an example of *phoresy*. Most birds are afflicted by such lice but their effects are not usually

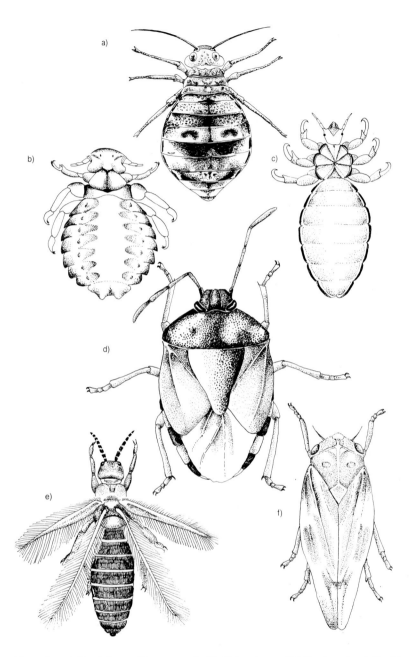

Fig. 16.4. a) Book-louse (Psocoptera). b) Biting-louse (Mallophaga). c) Sucking-louse (Siphunculata). d) Shield-bug (Hemiptera: Heteroptera). e) Thrips (Thysanoptera). f) Froghopper (Hemiptera: Homoptera).

195

severe, although those bird-lice that infest domestic poultry sometimes occur in such numbers as to induce considerable irritation and scratching, which in turn may cause secondary infection. Zoologically, bird-lice are of considerable interest since they show a high degree of host-specificity, the same or closely related species being found on phylogenetically related hosts. Evidence of this sort has led to revised ideas of bird relationships and classification. For example, the New Zealand kiwi is now thought to have a closer relationship to the rails and the flamingoes to ducks and geese – at least partly because they share similar lice.

Sucking-lice – Siphunculata (Latin *siphunculus* little pipe or siphon) *c.* 300 species. Worldwide. Fig. 16.4

Wingless like the preceding order, sucking-lice have piercing mouthparts for sucking the blood of their hosts, which range through a variety of mammals, including man. Usually with a rather small head and short antennae, they have strong curved legs armed at the tip with a single claw (two in Mallophaga) for clinging to the host's skin or hair. Like other blood-suckers, they inject saliva containing an anti-coagulant when they feed. Nearly every known mammal species is infested with some species of sucking-louse (bats appear to be an exception). Some even infest marine mammals, such as seals, walruses and whales, as they are able to tolerate long periods of immersion by taking down a layer of air trapped between modified body hairs or scales or by breathing air retained beneath the host's own hairs. In seal-lice, reproduction may be timed to coincide with the seals' own breeding on land. One of the best-known members of the Siphunculata is the notorious human-louse (*Pediculus humanus*), which occurs in two distinct races – *P. humanus capitis*, found only in the hair of the head (the tubular eggs, or 'nits' being affixed to hairs) and *P. humanus corporis* on the trunk. Increased hygiene has reduced human-louse infestation, although outbreaks are still likely to occur in crowded uncleanly conditions. Lice are also carriers of diseases such as typhus and relapsing fever but, like all blood-sucking insects, they need to feed on an already diseased host in order to effect their spread to healthy hosts.

Bugs – Hemiptera (Greek *hemi* half; *pteron* wing) *c.* 56 000 species. Worldwide. Fig. 16.4

This large order is divided into two suborders, the Homoptera and Heteroptera (sometimes recognised as orders), both of which have their mouthparts in the form of a sucking rostrum of varying length, which is usually partly sheathed beneath the head and thorax when not in use. Homoptera include the cicadas, leafhoppers, froghoppers, aphids, scale-insects, treehoppers, lantern-flies, lac-insects etc. They are characterised principally by the structure of their wings which are either uniformly textured or with the forepair wholly strengthened as covers for the membranous underpair. Heteroptera differ in having their forewings partly chitinised except for the tips which, together with the ends of the underwings, protrude when the insects fold their overlapping tegmina over the abdomen and present a characteristic appearance. Bugs are suckers of plant or animal tissues, although Homopterans are almost invariably vegetarian. Some of them, such as aphids and scale-insects, are of considerable economic importance because their sucking activities may cause the wilting and death of flowers and fruits as well as transmitting virus infections. Among the most interesting Homoptera are the tree-hoppers (Membracidae), which display an amazing variety of shapes and colours, often of a cryptic or other prey-deterring kind. Lantern-flies (Fulgoridae) are equally bizarre, with snout-like extensions of the head which, in the Brazilian *Laternaria*, is not unlike that of an alligator. Cicadas, which sometimes attain a considerable size, are best known for their ability to produce sounds, primarily for courtship or female-attracting purposes. These vary in character, some being harsh and penetrating, others more subtle and evanescent. Many Homopterid bugs are able to produce copious amounts of wax, often as a protective covering while feeding; in the Indian lac-insect (*Laccifera lacca*), the wax has long been used for making shellac. The Heteroptera are equally diverse. Large numbers of them, such as damsel-bugs, assassin-bugs, bed-bugs, water-scorpions, saucer-bugs and backswimmers etc, are predators or blood-suckers. Others, notably the tiny lacebugs, are wholly vegetarian, while still more (e.g. Capsids, Lygaeids, shield-bugs) may be either predatory or herbivorous or sometimes both. Many predatory species have their forelegs specially adapted for seizing prey. Apart from the bed-bug (*Cimex lectularius*), a number of other Heteroptera suck the blood of man, among them the South American *Rhodnius prolixus*. A feature of many Heteroptera is the care the female shows for her young. Usually this takes place without the help of the male, although an unusual example of parental solicitude is displayed by the huge 110–120 mm ($4\frac{1}{2} - 4\frac{3}{4}$ in) toe-biters or giant water-bugs, such as the North American *Lethocerus grandis*. In this case, the female deposits her eggs on the male's tegmina and the latter carries them about with him until they hatch. Giant water-bugs, which belong to the family Belostomatidae, are found in America, Africa and southern Asia.

Thrips or Bladder-Feet – Thysanoptera (Greek *thusanos* a fringe; *pteron* wing) *c.* 5000 species. Worldwide. Fig. 16.4

Often called 'thunder-flies' because of their tendency to be especially active in hot, thundery weather, flying and settling on people's arms, thrips are minute insects whose scientific name derives from the fringe of fine hairs which border each edge of the narrow wings, giving them a feathery appearance. Rather like tiny rove-beetles in appearance (there are Staphylinidae of this size), thrips have bladder-like organs at the ends of the legs instead of tarsal claws; these help the insects to gain purchase on smooth surfaces and are probably the cause of the tickling sensation when they alight on the body. Thrips feed mostly in flower heads and other vegetation by means of·sap-sucking mouthparts and some are minor pests, such as the cosmopolitan greenhouse thrips (*Heliothrips haemorrhoidalis*) and onion thrips (*Thrips tabaci*); others are waste or fungus feeders or predators, and some induce gall formations. Most species are only a few millimetres long, although the Australian *Idolothrips spectrum*, first discovered by Charles Darwin during his voyage on the Beagle, is about 12 mm ($\frac{1}{2}$ in). Thrips exhibit a number of curious features. In the suborder Terebrantia, the mouthparts are asymmetrical, the left mandible being fully developed while the right is absent. Their life history, too, seems to place them midway between the Exopterygota and Endopterygota, since they undergo one, and sometimes two, inactive pupa-like stages prior to adult emergence.

ENDOPTERYGOTA These insects undergo a complete metamorphosis with a proper pupal stage and are also known as Holometabola.

Scorpion-Flies, Snow-Flies, Hanging-Flies – Mecoptera (Greek *mekon* length; *pteron* wing) *c.* 400 species. Widespread. Fig. 16.5
Members of this order have a curious downward extension of the head, somewhat like a bird's beak, at the end of which are tiny cutting mandibles for piercing and chewing food, which consists of living and dead insects and a variety of waste materials. Scorpion-flies (Panorpidae) are so-called because of the peculiar structure of the male's genital capsule, which is generally glossy red and shaped like a scorpion's sting; females lack this device and have a pointed tapering abdomen. They have long antennae and two pairs of large transparent wings, striped and spotted with dark brown or black, although they are comparatively weak fliers. Snow-flies (Boreidae) possess a beak-like extension of the head but otherwise are so different as to be removed from the Mecoptera by some authorities and given separate status. Apparently confined to Europe and North America, they are very small (*c.* 3–7 mm or $\frac{3}{25} - \frac{1}{4}$ in), the male lacking the scorpion-flies' genital capsule and the female sporting a distinctive upcurved ovipositor. They are usually most active in winter or early spring, commonly running and jumping over snow and moss in upland regions and looking not unlike tiny nymphal grass-hoppers or bush-crickets. In both sexes, the wings are atrophied and useless for flight, the male using his spine-like pair for gripping the female during copulation. Hanging-flies (Bittacidae) are almost equally distinctive. Occurring in southern Europe, North America, South Africa and Australia, they are not unlike craneflies in general appearance but have two pairs of wings and quite different habits. Hanging-flies are predators with a unique method of capturing their prey – seizing passing insects with their prehensile hind legs while hanging from vegetation by the forelegs. They can fly well and are usually found in rank vegetation at the edges of forests or in open grassland. The Mecoptera as a whole are probably the oldest of the fully metamorphosing insects and their fossil ancestors (Paramecoptera) are

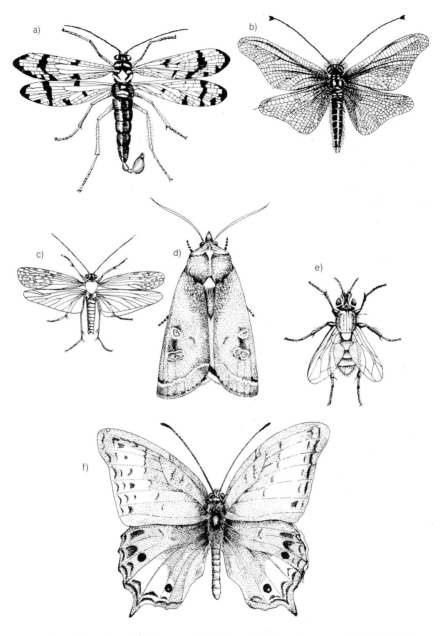

Fig. 16.5. a) Scorpion-fly (Mecoptera). b) Butterfly-lion (Neuroptera). c) Caddis-fly (Trichoptera). d) Moth (Lepidoptera). e) True fly (Diptera). f) Butterfly (Lepidoptera).

considered by many authorities to be the ancestors of several other insect orders including the Trichoptera (caddis flies), Lepidoptera (butterflies and moths), Diptera (true flies) and Siphonaptera (fleas). The Australian family Choristidae is of particular interest since its members are very similar to fossil species of the Permian period found in that country.

Alder-, Snake- and Mantis-Flies, Lacewings, Ant-Lions, etc – Neuroptera (Greek *neuron* nerve; *pteron* wing) *c.* 4000 species. Worldwide. Fig. 16.5

Members of this extremely diverse order vary individually but all have two pairs of large, membranous and intricately veined wings, commonly folded so as to form an arch over the body when the insects are at rest. Alder-flies and snake-flies comprise one of the group's two suborders (Megaloptera) but differ from each other in several respects. Alder-flies are dark, heavy-bodied insects with heads as wide as their bodies and dusky strongly veined wings. Their aquatic larvae are predatory, as are those of snake-flies, although the latter live under bark where they prey on the larvae of bark-beetles. Adult snake-flies gain their popular name from the shape of their elongated roughly triangular head and elongated prothorax, both of which are articulated in such a way as to present the appearance of a threatening cobra – an effect heightened in the female, who possesses a long needle-like ovipositor. Closely related are the large dobson-flies, found mainly in North America, males of which have huge mandibles, crossing at the tips, although these appear to serve no practical purpose. Dobson-fly larvae are aquatic predators and are colloquially called hellgrammites or toe-biters. One basic difference between the Megaloptera and members of the other suborder, the Planipennia, is that larvae of the former group chew their prey, whereas lacewing, ant-lion and mantis-fly larvae have hollow mandibles to assist in the pre-digestion and sucking out of their victims' tissues. Lacewing larvae commonly feed on aphids and scale-insects, some species camouflaging themselves with debris, including their own shed larval skins and the remains of victims; others of the group, such as *Osmylus*, are semi-aquatic as larvae, living in wet moss by rivers. Adult lacewings are delicate insects, often some shade of green or brown, commonly with pearly-iridescent wings, long antennae and prominent eyes which reflect light like garnets. Adult ant-lions, especially typical of arid or desert regions, are much larger insects, with distinctive hook-tipped antennae. They feed on small insects as well as nectar but their larvae are wholly predatory. Some build conical pits to trap their prey, while others lurk under stones or in sand to ambush their victims. Larvae of thread-lacewings (Nemopteridae) have a distinctive long narrow neck which enables them to lie in sand with only the head protruding. The adult thread lacewings gain their common name from their long ribbon-like underwings. Both they and the related butterfly-lions or owl-flies (Ascalaphidae) are predatory as adults, butterfly-lions having long simple antennae bearing a disc-like tip. Another interesting Planipennid family is the

Mantispidae or mantis-flies, adults of which have evolved a method of predation analogous to that of the true mantids. They have a greatly elongated prothorax and prehensile forelegs designed for seizing prey in almost precisely the same manner as mantids. Like mantids, too, they lie in wait for their victims in vegetation and flowers. Mantispid larvae live as parasites on other insects or spiders.

Caddis-Flies – Trichoptera (Greek *thrix* hair; *pteron* wing) *c.* 5 000 species. Worldwide. Fig. 16.5

Adults of this group look rather like dullish moths but have fine hairs on their wings, not the overlapping scales typical of Lepidoptera. They have long simple antennae and much reduced mouthparts, with the mandibles atrophied or absent, so that many do not feed or are capable only of lapping liquids such as tree sap and honeydew. Rarely found far from water, in which the larvae develop, adult caddis are not usually strong fliers, although some are occasionally attracted to artificial light. Caddis larvae are well known for their construction of protective cases, which are made of a variety of materials and often of a character distinctive of the family – bonded grains of sand, tiny complete shells, pieces of stick, reed, sometimes constructed in a spiral, in other instances lengthwise. Many species' cases are portable, the larva's head and legs protruding from the case's wider end with its body secured in the casing by terminal hooks. Others (e.g. Molannidae) construct immobile homes consisting of a tube bonded to a stone or other flat surface. Not all caddis larvae make cases, some being free-living; others, such as the Hydroptilidae, only construct them in their final instar. In all case-makers, pupation takes place within the case. A number of caddis larvae (e.g. *Hydropsyche*) are among the few insects to construct net traps for capturing prey, stretching a mesh of silk between rocks and then waiting nearby until the current washes victims into the web. Other larvae are vegetarian, feeding on algae and other minute plants, as well as decomposing plants. The adults' resemblance to moths is by no means fortuitous since caddis display a number of physical links with more primitive Lepidoptera, such as the Micropterigidae, notably in the sharing of a similar type of wing-coupling device used in flight, and in the fringed edges of the wings. Since the wing scales of moths and butterflies are essentially modified hairs, it seems likely that the Trichoptera and the Lepidoptera share a common ancestor.

Butterflies and Moths – Lepidoptera (Greek *lepis* scale; *pteron* wing) *c.* 160 000 species. Worldwide. Fig. 16.5

Until recently, science followed the popular practice of grouping this well-studied order into two divisions – the Rhopalocera (butterflies) and the Heterocera (moths). This, however, has been superseded and the whole order is now divided into four suborders. The butterflies comprise two superfamilies (Hesperoidea and Papilionoidea) and, together with the more advanced moths, make up the suborder Ditrysia; the more primitive moths are placed in the suborders Zeugloptera, Dacnonypha and Monotrysia. Structural and behavioural differences between butterflies and moths are anything but clear-cut and subject to so many contradictions that classification now more accurately reflects butterflies' relationships with moths, notably on the basis of wing venation and genitalia.

Typically Lepidoptera have two pairs of wings (although the females of some moths are wingless), covered with thousands of tiny overlapping scales of varying shape and colour, sometimes pigmented, sometimes arranged in such a way as to appear metallic or prismatic, as a result of light diffraction. The antennae may be club-ended (as in butterflies), ending in a hook (hawk-moths and burnets) or more usually simple and thread-like, sometimes bearing elaborate comb-like fringes along the edges. The mouthparts consist principally of a tubular proboscis, coiled up like a watchspring when not in use, for sucking nectar and other liquids. Some Lepidoptera (notably hawk-moths) have excessively long proboscides which enable them to probe the deep corollas of flowers and obtain nectar inaccessible to other insects. By contrast, certain primitive moths (Micropterigidae) lack a proboscis but have mandibles for chewing pollen. Some of the best-known butterfly families include the swallowtails and birdwings (Papilionidae), whites and sulphurs (Pieridae), monarchs, tigers and crows (Danaidae), browns (Satyridae), tortoiseshells, admirals, fritillaries, emperors, rajahs, map and leaf butterflies (Nymphalidae), blues, coppers and hairstreaks (Lycaenidae) and predominantly tropical groups such as the magnificent New World morphos (Morphidae), Heliconiidae, Amathusiidae, Ithomiidae, Acraeidae and Brassolidae. The last-mentioned include the intriguing owl butterflies which bear striking eye-like markings on their wings. Moths comprise about 90% of all Lepidoptera and are consequently even more diverse, ranging from tiny Microlepidoptera, such as leaf-miners, clothes-moths, yucca moths, bag-moths, plume-moths and torticids, to larger groups such as the wholly American 'horned devils' (Citheroniidae), emperors and silk-moths (Saturniidae), tigers (Arctiidae), tussocks (Lymantridae), hawk-moths (Sphingidae) and, perhaps the most beautiful of all Lepidoptera, the Uraniidae, which are represented in both the Old and New Worlds. *Chrysididia madagascariensis* is an especially magnificent member of the Uraniidae, being velvety black with bands of iridescent green, shading to orange and orange-red, the hindwings having white-edged tails. Many Lepidoptera are impressive fliers and some, such as Danaids, whites, Vanessids and hawk-moths habitually migrate for considerable distances.

The caterpillars of butterflies and moths are equally varied in appearance. Most have four or five pairs of pseudopodia, in addition to the three pairs just behind the head, although those of the Geometridae and some other families have only two pairs of hind claspers and are also commonly coloured and shaped so as to resemble twigs when clinging unmoving to their food plant. The majority feed on plant foliage, although a few consume wood (e.g. Cossidae) and others stored products, such as grain and woollens; a minority are carnivorous. Many caterpillars are brilliantly coloured or, as in the Lymantridae, armed with tufts of bristles that are easily shed and can cause severe skin irritation. Numbers of Lepidoptera, among them Zygaenid and Ctenuchid moths and Danaid and Heliconiid butterflies, are poisonous, both as adults and larvae, and are consequently avoided by predators such as birds. Lepidoptera vary in size from the very large to the exceedingly minute. Among giant species are the hercules moth (*Coscinocera hercules*), a member of the Saturniidae, from the tropical rain forests of Australia and New Guinea, with a reputed wingspan of up to 360 mm (14 in), and the tropical American Noctuid, *Thysania agrippina* (300 mm or 12 in). The smallest lepidopteran is probably the Tineid *Stigmella acetosae*, with a wing span of only 3–4 mm ($\frac{3}{25}-\frac{3}{25}$ in). Certain blue butterflies (*Brephidium*) from South Africa and North America are only about 14 mm ($\frac{1}{2}$ in) across the wings.

True Flies – Diptera (Greek *di* two; *pteron* wing) *c.* 85 000 species. Worldwide. Fig. 16.5

Many insect groups include 'fly' in their everyday name but entomologically the term should be applied only to the Diptera or true flies. Except for wingless species, all have only one pair of wings, the hind pair being replaced by often club-ended structures called halteres, which probably act as gyroscopic balancers in flight. The Diptera are arguably the most accomplished of all insect aeronauts, notably in their ability to fly backwards and forwards or tack sideways, often at great speed, as well as in their ability to remain on the wing when other insects are grounded through cold. Hoverflies, bee-flies and bot-flies are all particularly expert fliers and some of the former are able to migrate considerable distances – a remarkable feat in view of their size. Other Diptera, by contrast, are only feeble fliers, such as the long-legged craneflies or 'daddy-long-legs' (Tipulidae), whose larvae are the leatherjackets of agriculture. The curious Hippoboscidae and Nycteribiidae have abandoned flight altogether and live as ectoparasites of mammals and birds. The more typical winged dipteran adults feed in a variety of ways. The house-fly and related species (Muscidae), blowflies, bluebottles and green-bottles (Calliphoridae) and the fruit-flies (Drosophilidae) are principally saprophagous, with mouthparts consisting of a sponge-like haustellum through which liquids or pre-digested solids are sucked. Many others are blood-suckers or predators. Mosquitoes (Culicidae), biting-midges (Ceratopogonidae), tsetse-flies (Glossinidae), blackflies or buffalo gnats (Simulidae), horse-flies (Tabanidae), and some others, visit and suck the blood of various vertebrates, including man, at least partly to ensure the proper maturation of their eggs; in some cases, only the female has piercing mouthparts for this purpose. Robber-flies (Asilidae), some of which are large and impressive insects, fully capable of capturing small dragonflies, and snipe-flies (Rhagionidae) seize other insects in flight. A number of groups are endoparasitic in their larval stage, e.g. adult warble and bot-flies lay their

203

eggs on the skin of wild and domestic mammals and the larvae burrow into their flesh or make their way into the digestive tract. Since most dipteran larvae tend to live surrounded by their food, which is commonly of a liquid or semi-liquid nature, they are typically legless, although they range widely in their adaptations to particular feeding environments. Larvae of mosquitoes can swim readily, by means of doubling motions, breathing atmospheric air by means of a respiratory plate or terminal siphon and feeding on minute plants or animals. The rat-tailed maggot of the drone-fly (*Eristalis*) has a particularly long siphon which is to some extent telescopic. Both this and the bloodworm larvae of Chironomid midges live in or on mud at the bottom of the ponds. The midge larvae are unusual in possessing haemoglobin in their blood, and are thus capable of storing oxygen and existing in heavily polluted waters. Some fly larvae, such as those of hoverflies (Syrphidae), are entirely predacious, feeding on aphids and scale-insects. Other predatory larvae are among the very largest of the Diptera; they include the Neotropical Mydidae, whose larvae prey on the larvae of hercules beetles, which are themselves among the largest of all insects. Adults of the Brazilian *Mydas heros* have a wing-span of some 120 mm (nearly 5 in).

Fleas, Jiggers etc – Siphonaptera (Greek *siphon* a tube; Latin *a* without; Greek *pteron* wing) or **Aphaniptera** (Greek *aphanes* unapparent; *pteron* wing) *c.* 1 400 species. Worldwide. Fig. 16.6

Secondarily wingless, fleas are considered to be most closely related to the Diptera, some of which, as we have seen, are themselves wingless parasites. The adults are wholly parasitic, about 95% of species sucking the blood of terrestrial mammals, the remainder attacking birds. They are extremely well adapted to parasitic life, having toughened, laterally flattened bodies which help them to slip rapidly through their hosts' body hairs, as well as clawed legs and comb-like bristles on the body to aid the gripping of hairs and skin. The hind legs are long and powerful with enlarged coxae, well adapted for jumping from host to host. Vision is poor and the antennae short, although fleas are extremely sensitive to changes in body heat as well as to scent. By contrast with the adults, flea larvae are not blood-suckers but feed on skin debris as well as the imperfectly digested blood-rich excreta deposited by the adults in the host's lair. The larvae's sedentary nature tends to influence the adult fleas' preference for hosts with permanent homes, so that nomadic or free-ranging animals are less often infested. Many flea species are host-specific but, on the whole, rather less so than lice; the human flea (*Pulex irritans*), for example, also occurs on pigs and badgers and other species are not unwilling to transfer to quite different animals if necessary. It is possible that such flexibility indicates a fairly recent winged ancestry. A typical feature of the fleas' life history lies in their ability to survive long periods without feeding. Cat fleas (*Ctenocephalides felis*), for example, can exist almost indefinitely in uninhabited houses until new occupants arrive whereupon the resident flea larvae rapidly complete their development and

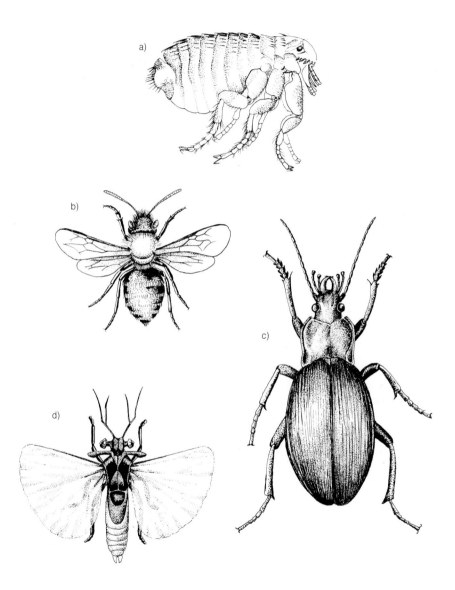

Fig. 16.6. a) Flea (Siphonaptera). b) Honey-bee (Hymenoptera). c) Ground-beetle (Coleoptera). d) Stylops (Strepsiptera).

emerge soon after their hosts' – cats or human beings – arrival. Like other parasitic insects, fleas feed by piercing the skin and injecting an anti-coagulant in their saliva. In so doing they may (as other parasites do) pass on pathogenic micro-organisms from host to host, one of the most serious being that causing bubonic plague which is carried by the Oriental rat flea (*Xenopsylla cheopis*). These fleas initially suck the blood of rats but, when the latter die, they transfer their attention to man. Infection is brought about because the alimentary canal of the flea often becomes congested with the parasites and, in clearing the obstruction, some of the diseased blood is passed into the wound. In the fourteenth and seventeenth centuries particularly, much of the population of Europe died as a result of plague or the 'Black Death' and there have been more recent epidemics in India and elsewhere. Other fleas carry less lethal infections but their parasitic effects can be highly unpleasant. Jiggers and stick-tight fleas (*Tunga, Echinophaga*) actually burrow into the flesh of animals and man and there may lay their eggs. One of the most noxious species is *Tunga penetrans*, which originates from South America but has spread to Africa and Asia. Burrowing into the feet and especially beneath the toenails of man, causing festering sores, it is among the very smallest of the Siphonaptera, being only a fraction of a millimetre long.

Bees, Wasps, Ants, Ichneumons, Sawflies etc – Hymenoptera (Greek *hymen* a membrane; *pteron* wing) *c.* 145 000 species. Worldwide. Fig. 16.6

The highly evolved social organisation of the honey- and bumble-bees, yellowjacket wasps and ants is known, at least in outline, to most non-entomologists. It is not, however, typical of the order as a whole because only a very small proportion of Hymenoptera are socially organised, and most lack a worker caste or exhibit only the beginnings of such behaviour. Of the two suborders, the Symphyta is by far the least numerous in species, comprising the so-called sawflies and the wood wasps or horntails. The second suborder, the Apocrita, includes the social and solitary bees, Vespoid wasps, ants and a wide variety of mainly parasitic groups, making up over 90% of the order. Symphyta are characterised by the lack of a waist between the thorax and abdomen, unlike the Apocrita. Sawflies gain their popular name from the shape of the females' ovipositor which has a serrated edge for the insertion of eggs into the plants on which the larvae feed, often in companies; the larvae often resemble the caterpillars of butterflies and moths except that they have more pseudopodia (six to eight pairs). Wood-wasps (Siricidae) possess an undifferentiated ovipositor, fitting into a sheath on the underside of the abdomen, for inserting eggs deep into the wood of the trees on which the larvae feed. A typical species is the large black and yellow *Urocerus gigas*. The 'wasp waist' of the Apocrita is less obvious in some groups than in others. In the ants, the area usually consists of one or more raised nodes. All true ants are socially organised, although driver- and army-ants (Dorylinae) do not make permanent nests; others make their homes in the ground, e.g. beneath mounds of soil, in the trunks of trees (e.g. *Camponotus*) or between leaves fastened together with larval silk (e.g. *Oecophylla*). Ants may be either carnivorous or herbivorous and are frequently both. Sight is not well developed, some worker castes being quite blind, while wings are only carried by queens and males. Unlike ants, which simply make chambers for their progeny's different developmental stages, honey-bees and social wasps construct hexagonal cells for their eggs and larvae; bumble-bees' egg-cells are more untidy affairs and are usually constructed in the ground. Many solitary bees also nest in the ground but vary enormously in habits. Those of the genus *Halictus*, a little like dark honey-bees in appearance, exhibit varying stages in social organisation, while others have no true workers, among them the well known leaf-cutter bees (Megachilidae), mason-bees (Andrenidae) and carpenter-bees (Xylocopidae). Solitary wasps also display many forms. Some of the most important of them are the ichneumon, Chalcid and Braconid 'flies', which lay their eggs in or on living caterpillars and other insects. Female ichneumons frequently possess ovipositors of enormous length, in some cases for parasitising horntail larvae. Other solitary wasps, including digger-wasps (Sphecidae) and spider-wasps (Pompilidae), provide for their young by storing subterranean cells with paralysed caterpillars or spiders. Cuckoo- or ruby-tailed wasps and so-called velvet-ants (Mutillidae) parasitise other members of the order; both are commonly brilliantly coloured, some cuckoo-wasps, for example, being metallic green or blue and red. Like many Hymenoptera, female velvet-ants have a powerful and painful sting, but this attribute is confined to the female (including the workers of social groups), since the sting is essentially a modification of the ovipositor. Many solitary Hymenoptera are extremely small, among them the Cynipidae which induce gall growths on various plants, especially oaks and roses, by laying their eggs in the leaf buds. Still more minute – indeed the smallest of all known insects – is *Alaptus magnanimus*, a Chalcid wasp a mere 0.2 mm ($\frac{7}{100}$ in) long, its diminutiveness allowing it to lay its eggs in those of booklice (Psocoptera).

Beetles – Coleoptera (Greek *coleos* sheath; *pteron* wing) *c.* 330 000 species. Worldwide. Fig. 16.6

The success of the insects is typified by the beetles, which are not merely the most numerous in species of all the insects but the largest order in the whole animal kingdom. They vary enormously in size, structure and habits, so that only a small proportion of them can be mentioned here. Typically they have their forewings wholly strengthened and chitinised as protective covers (elytra) for the operative under pair; in flight, the elytra are held up at an angle to allow the wings full play. Not all beetles are winged, however; some ground-beetles have their elytra fused, while others (especially females) are completely wingless and sedentary. Beetles may be predatory, herbivorous, omnivorous or waste-feeding and there is commonly a considerable difference in the diet of adults and larvae.

The hunters of the beetle world are the Carabidae, which include the ground-beetles and tiger-beetles, most being armed with powerful curved mandibles, both as adults and larvae. Other members of the family are the well-known bombardier beetles (*Brachinus*) which, like many beetles, can discharge an offensive secretion as a deterrent against enemies, the curious *Mormolyce* of Sumatra, which bears flat, leaf-like extensions at the sides of its body, and various aquatic species such as *Hygrobia* (screech-beetles). Allied to the Carabidae are the predatory diving-beetles (Dytiscidae), whirligig beetles (Gyrininae) and large water-beetles of the family Hydrophilidae, adults of which are waste-feeders in contrast to their wholly predatory larvae. Many of the extremely numerous rove-beetles (Staphylinidae) are also carnivorous, although others are scavengers. They are characterised by their very short waistcoat-like elytra, which, nevertheless, enclose large operative wings and they range in size from several centimetres long to tiny species which sometimes fly into the eye and cause irritation by their exudation of a defensive secretion. While many rove-beetles are drably tinted, others (e.g. *Paederus*) are highly coloured in blue and red, probably as a warning of distastefulness.

A feature of many beetle families is the difference in size and structure between the sexes – typified by the Lucanidae (stag-beetles), males of which sport large mandibles principally used for sexual display and jostling with rivals. The European stag-beetle (*Lucanus cervus*) is a well known example, but it is dwarfed by the 90 mm ($3\frac{1}{2}$ in) *Cladognathus giraffa* of Asia, whose vast jaws extend to almost half its body length. Another striking Lucanid is the New Guinea *Neolamprina adolphinae*, with lustrous green body, fiery red head and upcurved mandibles edged like a rip-saw. At the other end of the scale, the group also includes some very small species, such as the European *Sinodendron cylindricum*. Adult Lucanids are principally lappers of free liquids, whereas their larvae consume rotting wood and, like many such groups, may take several years to complete their development. Some of the world's largest beetles are members of the family Scarabaeidae, such as the huge goliath beetles of tropical Africa and the South American *Dynastes herculeanus* (hercules beetle), probably the longest beetle in the world (180 mm or 7 in) the males bearing vast forwardly directed horns on the thorax. The group also includes more modestly sized species such as the sacred scarab (*Scarabaeus sacer*), as well as the chafers which typically feed on roots in the larval stage. Many large species are also included in the Cerambycidae, or longhorn beetles, whose larvae bore into wood and structural timbers. The family is notable for the possession of unusually long, filiform antennae which, in species like *Acanthosoma aedilis* (timberman), may be several times the length of the body. Giants of the group include the South American *Titanus giganteus* (150 mm or 6 in long, excluding antennae) and the slightly smaller *Xixuthrus heyrovski* of Fiji, the huge larvae of which are eaten by local people as a delicacy. Other striking longhorns are *Acrocinus longimanus*, remarkable for its long forelegs, which probably help it to climb the fig trees in which its larvae develop, and species of *Macrodontia*, whose mandibles are untypically very long and saw-edged. Larvae of several other beetle families are wood-eaters and some of them can cause considerable damage to structural timbers, as well as furniture. They include the so-called wood-worms (Anobiidae), powderpost beetles (Lyctidae), bark and ambrosia beetles (Scolytidae) and the Bostrychidae, some of which have been known to gnaw through plastic and lead. Others, such as the Dermestidae, consume stored or man-made products. By contrast, the affectionately regarded ladybird beetles (Coccinellidae) are of value to man, both as adults and larvae, in consuming large numbers of aphids and scale-insects; the adults are predominantly red or yellow and black (typical aposematic colours). Some of the most beautifully coloured, if generally small, beetles belong to the families Buprestidae, Chrysomelidae and Curculionidae. Mainly trop-ical in distribution, Buprestids include the famous jewel-beetles, many of them displaying brilliant metallic greens, blues, violet and red. Leaf-beetles (Chrysomelidae), which include the tortoise and flea-beetles, are commonly no less colourful. Both are more than matched by the iridescent diamond-beetles (*Entimus* and related genera), which occur in South America and other tropical regions. They are members of the long-snouted weevil family (Curculionidae), all of which are plant-feeders and include some important consumers of cultivated crops and stored products.

Closely related to the weevils are the curiously stick-like Brenthidae, which are found mainly in the tropics. The well-known fireflies and glow-worms are also most typical of the tropics, although having a widespread distribution. They belong mainly to the families Lampyridae and Phen-godidae, although several large species belong to the Elateridae or click-beetles, some of which have 'wireworm' larvae injurious to agriculture. These beetles' aesthetically pleasing light, produced biochemically and usually of a brilliant greenish colour, is used as a sexual attractant. Life history in the Coleoptera follows the usual metamorphic pattern, although individually is subject to much variation. Some beetle families, for example, exhibit hypermetamorphosis. These include the oil-beetles and blister-beetles (Meloidae), some of which yield a substance called cantharidin, once used medicinally and as an aphrodisiac.

Stylopids – Strepsiptera (Greek *strepsis* pliant, twisted; *pteron* wing) *c.* 370 species. Worldwide. Fig. 16.6

At one time classified with beetles, Stylopids are among the most obscure and highly specialised of all insects. They are rarely seen because of their small size and endoparasitic lifestyle which, in the female, involves her never leaving her host. Male Stylopids are the more active sex, with relatively large fan-like underwings but no forewings, which are replaced by twisted rod-like structures which give the group their name; they also have large compound eyes and curiously forked antennae. Males fly well and rapidly, typically with the head and thorax vertical and the abdomen thrust forward, their wingbeats producing a hum like that of a tiny bee. Females are very different in form; legless, eyeless and without antennae, they live a totally sedentary life within the abdomen of various mainly solitary bees, as well as Homopteran bugs, Mantids, flies, grasshoppers etc. Here the female is visited by the tiny (up to 4 mm or $\frac{3}{20}$ in long) male and produces up to about 2000 eggs, which hatch into tiny active triungulin larvae. Such drastic internal interference does not seem to incapacitate the host unduly, so that when it subsequently visits flowers or vegetation, the Stylopid larvae are able to escape via a hole in the forepart of the carrier's abdomen. They then wait until a suitable insect host arrives, whereupon they burrow inside it to recommence the cycle once more. Several members of both sexes may occupy a single host, but whereas the males hatch from pupae and escape to visit other females, the latter remain larviform and die within their host's abdomen after producing eggs. As mentioned, the parasitised insect may remain relatively active despite the parasitisation, although it is commonly rendered sterile as the Stylopid often consumes part of the reproductive system. This sometimes produces curious effects, e.g. male hosts may exhibit female characters and vice versa.

Glossary

Aedegus Male insect's intromittent organ.

Aestivation Period of inactivity undergone during excessively hot, dry conditions; summer hibernation.

Alate Winged (Latin *ala*, wing); applied especially to sexual forms of e.g. ants, aphides.

Apterygota Literally 'without wings'; the four orders of wingless insects (Thysanura, Protura, Diplura, Collembola) which are wingless and seem to have descended from similarly wingless (i.e. primarily wingless) insects.

Arolium Small pad between the tarsal claws of the foot which together with the **pulvilli** *q.v.*, helps insects to move on very smooth surfaces.

Arthropoda Literally 'jointed limbs'; the phylum which includes the insects, crustaceans, centipedes, millipedes, spiders etc.

Chitin Tough, horny material forming the main constituent of the cuticle or **exoskeleton** *q.v.*

Cocoon Protective case, usually of silk, which contains the insect pupa.

Corbicula or **pollen basket**. Simple receptacle, found in bees, for collecting pollen; formed of rows of bristles on the hind legs.

Cryptic camouflage Colour pattern, displayed by many insects, enabling them to merge with their surroundings.

Diapause Any period of suspended development, e.g. in **hibernation** or **aestivation** *q.v.*; may occur in the egg, larval (nymphal) or pupal stages.

Ecdysis Process of shedding the outer cuticle during development or **metamorphosis** *q.v.*

Eclosion Emergence of larva (nymph) from the egg, or adult from the full-grown nymph or pupa.

Exoskeleton Hardened outer cuticle of an insect.

Exuviae (always plural). Shed cuticle of an insect.

Frenulum Bristle, or group of bristles, on the leading edge of the hind wing of moths and some butterflies; it engages in a retaining device or **retinaculum** on the forewing, enabling the wings to operate together in flight.

Furcula Forked device at the tip of the abdomen of springtails enabling them to jump.

Gall Abnormal plant growth resulting from feeding activities of insect larvae or nymphs.

Genetic altruism Instinctive, inheritable parental care of the young; displayed by social insects, and some beetles, bugs, earwigs.

Haemolymph Sea of liquid surrounding an insect's internal organs; insect 'blood'.

Halteres Pair of club-ended structures which replace the hind wings in Diptera and act as gyroscopic balancers during flight.

Hexapoda Literally 'six-legged'; an alternative name for the class Insecta.

Hibernation Period of inactivity or delayed development during cold conditions.

Imago Perfect adult insect.

Instar Any larval (or nymphal) stage between two **ecdyses** q.v.; thus a newly hatched larva is in its first instar, after the first ecdysis in its second instar, and so forth.

Invertebrate Somewhat loose term applied to any animal lacking a vertebral column, e.g. an insect, spider etc.

Johnston's organ Structure at the base of many insects' antennae which interprets information received by the latter and may be concerned with vibration, gravitational balance, etc.

Larva Active, juvenile form of a Holometabolous insect, e.g. butterfly, beetle, fly (see Metamorphosis).

Metamorphosis Literally 'change of shape': the life history or development of an insect from egg to adult, involving radical structural changes from one stage to the next. In insects undergoing **complete metamorphosis** (Holometabola or Endopterygota), the sequence is egg-larva-pupa-adult. In those displaying **incomplete metamorphosis** (Hemimetabola or Exopterygota), there is no proper pupal stage: adults emerge from full-grown larvae, generally called **nymphs** (q.v.) to distinguish them from the first group. In insects undergoing **hypermetamorphosis**, there is an apparent additional larval (or pre-pupal) stage when the larva changes its form radically as a result of altered feeding circumstances.

Mimicry Of two types. **Batesian mimicry** is the imitation by a generally innocuous insect of a poisonous, stinging or otherwise well-armed model. In **Müllerian mimicry**, two or more equally poisonous or distasteful insects share the same warning patterns and thus mutually benefit, since predators have only to learn to avoid them once.

Nymph Active, feeding, growing stage of a Hemimetabolous insect, e.g. grasshopper, dragonfly (see **Metamorphosis**).

Ommatidium Single facet of an insect's compound eye.

Ootheca Egg-capsule, produced by insects such as mantids, cockroaches, usually consisting of a spongy mass in which the eggs are embedded.

Parthenogenesis Reproduction by means of the unfertilised egg; typical of the social insects, aphides, etc. but a potential of a great many others.

Pheromone Largely olfactory chemical substance which may be exuded by insects of both sexes as a sexual attractant or for social bonding purposes.

Pulvilli Pair of small pads between the tarsal claws of many insects which enable them to grip smooth surfaces (see **Arolium**).

Puparium A protective case for the pupa derived from the last larval **exuviae** *q.v.*, typical of certain Diptera or true flies.

Retinaculum see **Frenulum.**

Rostrum Usually piercing, sucking mouthparts, especially typical of Hemiptera (bugs). The term 'proboscis' has a wider application to include simple sucking (or non-piercing) mouthparts, e.g. in liquid-consuming butterflies and moths.

Sclerotin A proteinous substance which, with **chitin** *q.v.*, forms the hard protective cuticle of insects.

Sexual dimorphism The difference in shape, structure and colour displayed by many male and female insects of the same species.

Taxonomy The scientific naming and classifying of animals and plants.

Tegmen (pl. **tegmina**) Semi-operative forewing of insects such as grass-hoppers and phasmids.

Telson An additional terminal abdominal segment present in many insect larvae but in adults found only in the primitive Protura; used in locomotion or as a balancing aid.

Teneral An adult insect whose cuticle has not yet hardened fully or whose colours are not wholly apparent.

Thigmotaxis A tendency to press the body against a surface or into a corner.

Triungulin larva Active larvae of certain insects, e.g. oil-beetles, which are carried to their nests on the legs and bodies of certain bees and there undergo **hypermetamorphosis**. The name derives from the three claws at the tip of the larva's legs.

Tymbals Pair of membranes used for producing communicative courtship sounds in cicadas.

Tympanum (pl. **tympani**) One of a pair of membranes which receives and vibrates in response to sounds; especially typical of courting crickets, grasshoppers and cicadas, but also present in some moths.

Zoogeographical region Area regarded as a unit because of broad similarities in its animal fauna, indicating common evolutionary origins, although such regions' boundaries are far from being clear-cut.

Guide to Further Reading

General Works

Blaney, W.M. (1976) *How Insects Live* Elsevier-Phaidon, Oxford.
A popular, well illustrated short account of the subject.

Chapman, R.F. (1982) *The Insects: Structure and Function* 3rd edition. Hodder & Stoughton, Sevenoaks, Kent.
Detailed advanced study.

Friedlander, C.P. (1976) *The Biology of Insects* Hutchinson, London.
Short undergraduate-level text, with especially useful sections on evolution and economic and medical aspects.

Grzimek, B. (1975) *Grzimek's Animal Life Encyclopedia*, Vol. 2: *Insects* Van Nostrand Reinhold, Wokingham, Berkshire.
A descriptive account of the insect orders.

Imms, A.D. (1971) *Insect Natural History* 3rd edition. Collins, London.
British bias but one of the best popular introductions to the subject.

Imms, A.D. (1978) *Outlines of Entomology* 6th edition. Chapman & Hall, London.
As revised by O.W. Richards and R.G. Davies; a basic text for serious students.

Klots, A.B. & Klots, E.B. (1959) *Living Insects of the World* Hamish Hamilton, London.
Well illustrated descriptive account of the orders.

Linsenmaier, W. (1972) *Insects of the World* McGraw-Hill, Maidenhead, Berkshire.
A very well illustrated popular account, with details of the insect orders and all aspects of their structure and behaviour.

Stanek, V.J. (1969) *The Pictorial Encyclopaedia of Insects* Hamlyn, Feltham, Middlesex.
With nearly 1000 photos in halftone and colour, useful for getting the 'feel' of insect variety.

Wigglesworth, V.B. (1964) *The Life of Insects*. Weidenfeld & Nicolson, London.
A popular study of insect biology and behaviour.

Special Aspects

Askew, R.R. (1971) *Parasitic Insects* Heinemann, London.

Busvine, J.R. (1966) *Insects and Hygiene* 2nd edition. Methuen, London.
Insects that bite, carry disease, etc.

Ford, R.L.E. (1973) *Studying Insects* Warne, London.
Practical aspects of the subject, with emphasis on collecting but with good advice on seeking, attracting and rearing insects.

Haskell, P.T. (1961) *Insect Sounds* Witherby, London.

Hollis, D. (ed.) (1980) *Animal Identification – a Reference Guide* Vol. 3: *Insects* British Museum (Natural History), London/John Wiley, Chichester.
Merely a comprehensive compilation of references to specialist texts and papers for the identification of insects worldwide, but quite invaluable for the serious researcher.

Nachtigall, W. (1974) *Insects in Flight* Allen & Unwin, London.
A mildly turgid translation from the German, but the best semi-popular account of insect aerodynamics.

Oldroyd, H. (1970) *Collecting, Preserving and Studying Insects* 2nd edition. Hutchinson, London.
A very useful practical text, with especially valuable information on the principles of insect naming and classification, recording observations, new species, etc.

Smart, J. (1965) *A Handbook for the Identification of Insects of Medical Importance* 4th edition. British Museum (Natural History), London.

Tweedie, M. (1968) *Pleasure from Insects* David & Charles, Newton Abbot, Devon.
Quite the most appealing practical guide to insect study.

Williams, C.B. (1966) *Insect Migration* Collins, London.

Wigglesworth, V.B. (1974) *The Principles of Insect Physiology* 7th edition. Chapman & Hall, London.
A good basic text.

Index

Numbers in *italics* refer to black and white illustrations.
Numbers in **bold** refer to colour plates.